THE RESERVATIONS

TIME® LIFE BOOKS

Other Publications
THE TIME-LIFE COMPLETE GARDENER
THE NEW HOME REPAIR AND IMPROVEMENT
JOURNEY THROUGH THE MIND AND BODY
WEIGHT WATCHER® SMART CHOICE RECIPE COLLECTION
TRUE CRIME
THE ART OF WOODWORKING
LOST CIVILIZATIONS
ECHOES OF GLORY
THE NEW FACE OF WAR
HOW THINGS WORK
WINGS OF WAR
CREATIVE EVERYDAY COOKING
COLLECTOR'S LIBRARY OF THE UNKNOWN
CLASSICS OF WORLD WAR II
TIME-LIFE LIBRARY OF CURIOUS AND UNUSUAL FACTS
AMERICAN COUNTRY
VOYAGE THROUGH THE UNIVERSE
THE THIRD REICH
MYSTERIES OF THE UNKNOWN
TIME FRAME
FIX IT YOURSELF
FITNESS, HEALTH & NUTRITION
SUCCESSFUL PARENTING
HEALTHY HOME COOKING
UNDERSTANDING COMPUTERS
LIBRARY OF NATIONS
THE ENCHANTED WORLD
THE KODAK LIBRARY OF CREATIVE PHOTOGRAPHY
GREAT MEALS IN MINUTES
THE CIVIL WAR
PLANET EARTH
COLLECTOR'S LIBRARY OF THE CIVIL WAR
THE EPIC OF FLIGHT
THE GOOD COOK
WORLD WAR II
THE OLD WEST

*For information on and a full description of any of the Time-Life Books
series listed above, please call 1-800-621-7026 or write:*
Reader Information
Time-Life Customer Service
P.O. Box C-32068
Richmond, Virginia 23261-2068

This volume is one of a series that chronicles the history and culture of the Native Americans. Other books in the series include:

THE FIRST AMERICANS
THE SPIRIT WORLD
THE EUROPEAN CHALLENGE
PEOPLE OF THE DESERT
THE WAY OF THE WARRIOR
THE BUFFALO HUNTERS
REALM OF THE IROQUOIS
THE MIGHTY CHIEFTAINS
KEEPERS OF THE TOTEM
CYCLES OF LIFE

WAR FOR THE PLAINS
TRIBES OF THE SOUTHERN WOODLANDS
THE INDIANS OF CALIFORNIA
PEOPLE OF THE ICE AND SNOW
PEOPLE OF THE LAKES
THE WOMAN'S WAY
INDIANS OF THE WESTERN RANGE
HUNTERS OF THE NORTHERN FOREST
TRIBES OF THE SOUTHERN PLAINS

The Cover: The four generations of a Lakota family, shown in this 1906 photograph taken on the Rosebud Reservation in South Dakota, symbolize the changes imposed on the reservation Indians by the U.S. government. Two Strike, seated on the ground holding his great-granddaughter, and his son Little Hawk—in war bonnet—wear largely traditional clothing. But his grandson Poor Boy, holding the American Flag, and the baby are dressed in the manner of whites.

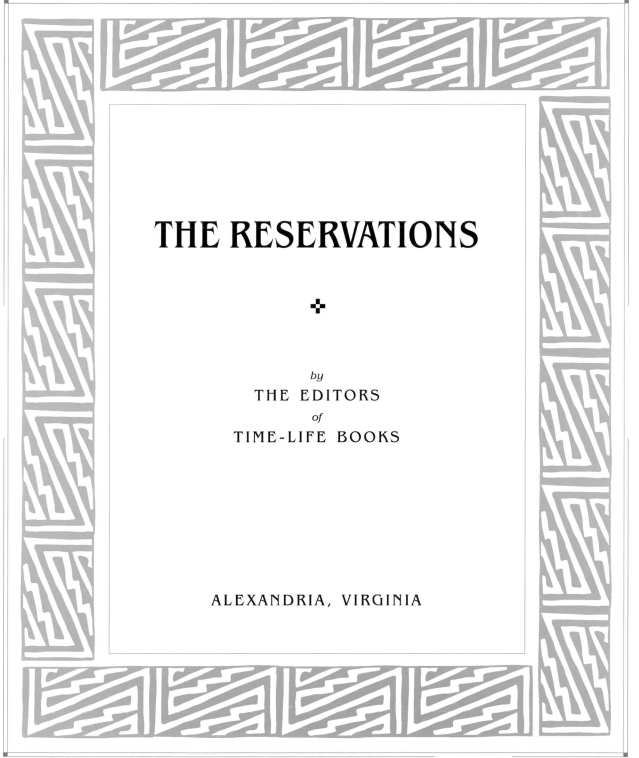

THE RESERVATIONS

✛

by
THE EDITORS
of
TIME-LIFE BOOKS

ALEXANDRIA, VIRGINIA

Time-Life Books is a division of Time Life Inc.

PRESIDENT and CEO: John M. Fahey Jr.

TIME-LIFE BOOKS

MANAGING EDITOR: Roberta Conlan

Director of Design: Michael Hentges
Director of Editorial Operations: Ellen Robling
Director of Photography and Research: John Conrad Weiser
Senior Editors: Russell B. Adams Jr., Dale M. Brown, Janet Cave, Lee Hassig, Robert Somerville, Henry Woodhead
Special Projects Editor: Rita Thievon Mullin
Director of Technology: Eileen Bradley
Library: Louise D. Forstall

PRESIDENT: John D. Hall

Vice President, Director of Marketing: Nancy K. Jones
Vice President, Director of New Product Development: Neil Kagan
Vice President, Book Production: Marjann Caldwell
Production Manager: Marlene Zack
Quality Assurance Manager: Miriam P. Newton

THE AMERICAN INDIANS

SERIES EDITOR: Henry Woodhead
Administrative Editor: Loretta Y. Britten

Editorial Staff for *The Reservations*
Senior Art Director: Ray Ripper
Picture Editor: Susan V. Kelly
Text Editor: John Newton (principal), Denise Dersin, Stephen G. Hyslop
Associate Editors/Research-Writing: Trudy W. Pearson (principal), Mary Helena McCarthy, Jennifer Veech
Senior Copyeditor: Ann Lee Bruen
Picture Coordinator: Daryl Beard
Editorial Assistant: Christine Higgins

Special Contributors: Ronald H. Bailey, William Clark, Marge duMond, Jim Hicks, Tom Lewis, David S. Thomson (text); Marilyn Murphy Terrell (research-writing); Martha Lee Beckington, Barbara Fleming, Barbara L. Klein, Carla Reissman (research); Julie Sherman Grayson (index).

Correspondents: Christine Hinze (London), Christina Lieberman (New York). Maria Vincenza Aloisi (Paris). Valuable assistance was also provided by: Elizabeth Brown (New York), Carolyn Sackett (Seattle).

General Consultant
Frederick E. Hoxie is vice president for research and education at the Newberry Library in Chicago and former director of its D'Arcy McNickle Center for the History of the American Indian. Dr. Hoxie is the author of *A Final Promise: The Campaign to Assimilate the Indians 1880-1920* (1984) and *Parading Through History: The Making of the Crow Nation in America, 1805-1935* (1995), and editor of *Indians in American History* (1988) and *Discovering America* (1994). He has served as a history consultant to the Cheyenne River Sioux tribe, the Little Big Horn College archives, and the Select Committee on Indian Affairs of the U.S. Senate. He is a founding trustee of the Smithsonian Institution's National Museum of the American Indian in Washington, D.C.

First printing. Printed in U.S.A.
Published simultaneously in Canada.
School and library distribution by Time-Life Education, P.O. Box 85026, Richmond, Virginia 23285-5026.
Time-Life is a trademark of Time Warner Inc. U.S.A.

Library of Congress Cataloging in Publication Data
The reservations/by the editors of Time-Life Books.
    p. cm.—(The American Indians)
    Includes bibliographical references and index.
    ISBN 0-8094-9737-9
    1. Indian reservations—History. 2. Indians of North America—Land tenure. 3. Indians of North America—Government relations. 4. Indians, Treatment of—North America. I. Time-Life Books.
II. Series.
E91.R47 1995   95-4967
333.2—dc20   CIP

CONTENTS

1
ENCLAVES TO PRESERVE THE PEOPLE

2
WALKING THE WHITE MAN'S ROAD

3
THE STRUGGLE FOR INDIAN RIGHTS

ESSAYS

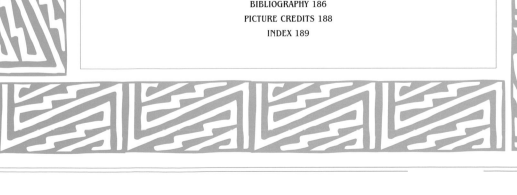

"CIVILIZING" THE INDIANS

During the last quarter of the 19th century, thousands of young Indians were taken off their reservations and sent to federally supported boarding schools in an effort to assimilate them into white society.

The idea originated with Richard Henry Pratt, a career army officer who had been placed in charge of 72 Plains tribesmen incarcerated at Fort Marion, Florida, for their alleged roles in the Red River War. In 1878 Pratt asked his friend Samuel Chapman Armstrong to accept 17 of the former prisoners at Hampton Normal and Agricultural Institute, which Armstrong had opened a decade earlier for the education of black freedmen. The Hampton program became the forerunner of some two dozen schools, including the Carlisle Indian Industrial School founded by Pratt in 1879 in Carlisle, Pennsylvania. At Carlisle, as at the other schools, the Indians were im-

mersed in courses of English, arithmetic, farming, and other vocational skills. But the ultimate goal was nothing less than to eradicate native ways and values, or, as Pratt himself put it, to "kill the Indian and save the man."

The first step at all the schools was invariably the exchange of native garb for the clothes of mainstream America and a haircut for all the males. Dramatic "before" and "after" photographs, such as those shown here and on the following pages, were used to demonstrate success at "civilizing" the Indians. But the goal was never achieved quite as white educators had envisioned it. Instead of forgetting their tribal ties, many of the Indians came away with a strengthened sense of identity, a voice in which to better communicate with one another, and a mastery of the skills needed to fight for Indian rights in a white-dominated world.

Tom Torlino, a Navajo from Arizona, wore tribal headgear, earrings, and a necklace (above) upon his arrival at the Carlisle Indian School. A few years later (right), he appears with close-cropped hair wearing a suit and tie.

Newly arrived at the Carlisle Indian School, these Sioux boys were permitted to keep their tribal outfits only long enough for this picture to be taken. The photograph at right shows them wearing their school uniforms.

Wrapped in blankets, a solemn group of little girls huddle together upon their arrival at the government school in Santa Fe, New Mexico, in 1886. One week later (right), they posed in calico dresses and straw hats.

These boys from various Plains tribes were photographed at Hampton Institute shortly after their arrival and again 15 months later (right). African American educator Booker T. Washington, who helped the Indians adjust to life at Hampton, recalled: "The things they disliked the most were to have their long hair cut, to give up wearing their blankets, and to cease smoking. But no white American ever thinks that any other race is wholly civilized until he wears the white man's clothes, eats the white man's food, speaks the white man's language, and professes the white man's religion."

1

ENCLAVES TO PRESERVE THE PEOPLE

An 18th-century Huron (Wyandot) chief displays a wampum belt, a traditional instrument of diplomacy. Icons woven into the pattern of colored shell beads commemorate key events. The belt above, linking an Indian to a white man, was probably used to renew the pledge of friendship between the Iroquois and the British.

In the years immediately prior to that signal moment in American history when Myles Standish and the other Pilgrim Fathers stepped from their boat onto an alien shore in 1620, the native inhabitants of the region that would become New England faced a catastrophe of epic proportions. A mysterious epidemic brought to the forests of the American Northeast by European seafarers swept through the Indian settlements from the Saco River in southern Maine to the Quinnipiac River in western Connecticut. The disease—probably smallpox or plague—destroyed entire communities, wiping out perhaps 90 percent of a population that may have ranged as high as 144,000 before the pestilence struck. Among the hardest hit were the Massachusett, an important Algonquian-speaking people who lived in more than 20 villages along the shore of the present-day state to which the Indians would lend their name. It meant "around the great hill," a reference to the site of a principal village below the wooded highlands where the modern city of Milton, Massachusetts, just south of Boston, would arise.

In the early 1600s, the Massachusett had been a force to be reckoned with, numbering perhaps 24,000 people. By the time the Puritans landed in 1620, however, fewer than 1,000 remained. Yet even this weakened, disease-racked remnant outnumbered the white intruders, and without the goodwill of the Massachusett and other southern New England tribes, the Puritans might never have established a foothold—just as the first English settlement in the New World some 30 years earlier, on Roanoke Island off the coast of present-day North Carolina, failed to take root after the local Indians turned against it.

Almost from the beginning, the fortunes of the Massachusett and the Puritans moved in opposite directions. Soon the colonists had broken their dependence on Indian generosity and no longer needed the Indians' expertise in gardening, hunting, fishing, or woodcraft. The Indians, on the other hand, grew increasingly reliant on European trade goods and began to adjust their subsistence ways to fit the new reality of the permanent

Some Plains Indians recorded significant events by drawing pictographs on a piece of hide. The ones at right, drawn by Sioux from various groups, depict (from left) death by measles, whooping cough, smallpox, starvation, dropsy, and cholera—afflictions introduced to their communities by whites.

English presence. They began fencing off their cornfields to adapt to English notions of property and participated in the colonial economy by selling excess venison, wild turkeys, fish, cranberries, and other foodstuffs in Puritan markets. Some mastered new crafts, learning to make brooms, baskets, and wooden staves to sell or trade to the Puritans. Others hired out as laborers.

As the English population multiplied, the population of Indians withered. By the mid-1640s, the number of residents in the Massachusetts Bay Colony approached 20,000, while the total number of settlers in all of New England surpassed 50,000. Meanwhile the once powerful Massachusett, weakened by another epidemic of smallpox, had shrunk to fewer than 500 men, women, and children. Operating from radically different cultural perspectives, both the Indians and the English sought remedies to what was fast becoming an apocalyptic crisis for the surviving members of the tribe.

In November 1646 legislators of the Massachusetts Bay Colony voted to create a new kind of community "for the incuragement of the Indians to live in an orderly way amongst us." The spiritual architect of this idea was John Eliot, the 42-year-old minister of the First Church of Roxbury and the colony's most prominent Puritan missionary. Eliot was convinced that the New England Indians were descendants of the lost tribes of Israel. He was so determined to convert them to Christianity that he mastered their language and spent his spare time translating catechisms, psalters, primers, grammars, and, of course, the Bible into the Massachusett dialect. Eliot believed that by living like Englishmen and worshiping like Puritans the Indians would be "reduced to civility." This would be in keeping with the colony charter, which vowed to "wynn and incite the Natives of [the] country, to the Knowledge and Obedience of the onlie true God and Savior of Mankinde, and the Christian Fayth."

For a variety of reasons, most of the Massachusetts cooperated, at least outwardly. When asked why he prayed to the Christian God, one convert explained, "Because I saw the English took much ground, and I thought if I prayed, the English would not take away my ground." Reeling from their terrible setbacks, many Indians had lost faith in the spiritual powers of their medicine men, or powwows as they called them (an Algonquian word that would eventually enter the English language as a term for any Indian gathering). Since the arrival of the white man, the old sacred ways no longer seemed to work as they had in the past, and some

Indians saw the religion of the newcomers as a panacea for their misfortunes. Most of them, however, submitted to the Puritans as a means to helping themselves build a new life—one that would allow them to retain as many threads of their traditional values and practices as possible.

In 1651 the town of Natick was established on 6,000 acres for Christian Indians. The Massachusett helped to select the site. It encompassed one of their former villages of the same name and a patch of sacred planting ground they had gardened "even beyond the memory of the oldest man alive." The entire area had previously been incorporated into the English town of Dedham, but Eliot's strong advocacy persuaded the Dedham elders to return it to the Indians.

Colonial carpenters helped the Massachusett Indians build their new community. It boasted three broad streets, a large meeting house, orchards, and plowed fields enclosed by fences. Several individual lots had square-timbered frame houses with stone chimneys. Along with these outward aspects of a typical English town, however, the Indians kept a vestige of their former life by erecting wigwams, which they found more comfortable than their drafty English-style homes.

Eliot gave shape to what he called a Christian Commonwealth. Promising to "fly to the Scriptures, for every Law, Rule, Direction, Form, or what ever we do," he extracted from the Book of Exodus a hierarchical scheme in which elected Indian leaders would supervise groups of 10, 50, and 100 of their people. Elements of Eliot's structure resembled the Massachusett's own leadership system. As with most eastern Algonquians, their civil leadership came from a hierarchy of sachems, or chiefs, from high-ranking families. They put their stamp on the Natick arrangement by electing their principal sachem, Cutshamekin, as ruler of the groups of 100, and making Waban, another ranking sachem, the ruler of the 50s. Lesser sachems, in turn, became rulers of the groups of 10. Ultimate political control of Natick, however, rested with Eliot and the other Puritans.

The Indians of Natick clung to as many aspects of their former ways as the Puritans would tolerate. Many of them equated the Puritan requirement of daily prayer and regular worship services with their own daily rituals for bountiful crops, game animals, fish, and wild plants. The major Christian holidays fit nicely with the Indian pattern of seasonal ceremonies that maintained the reciprocal relationship between the natural world and the world of the spirits.

The Indians also had to accept new strictures, however. They were compelled to comply with the Massachusetts Bay Colony's strict legal code as well as with local laws that were specifically designed for Natick by Eliot. One law, for example, forbade the Indians to perform "outward worship to their false gods, or to the devil." All customs and habits that conflicted with biblical injunctions or English prejudices were banned. These included gambling, polygamy, and premarital sexual relations. The Indians were also pressured to anglicize their names. And before the English allowed them to establish a church, they had to prove before an examining board of Puritan elders that they possessed a substantial knowledge of the Scriptures and Calvinist doctrine.

The Indians themselves regulated how they dressed. Males usually preferred traditional clothing—deerskin moccasins, leather leggings attached to leather breechcloth, and mantle of bearskin or a blanket. But some Natick residents adopted European dress as a means of winning the acceptance of the Puritans and their God. Hair style was another matter. Traditionally, some warriors wore the left side of their hair long and the right side short to accommodate their drawn bowstrings; others shaved their heads entirely except for a circular scalp lock of long braided hair on the crown. Eliot, whose goals were to "convince, bridle, restrain, and civilize" Indians—"and also to humble them"—seized upon hair as a symbol of male pride and forced the men to cut it. "They will weare their haire comely," stated one town law, "as the English do."

Eliot also wrote a series of imaginary dialogues to help train Natick residents as missionaries for work among other Indians. In these contrived conversations, which were designed to dispel skepticism, he sometimes unwittingly pinpointed uncomfortable truths. In one dialogue, for example, the Indian asks: "May not we rather think that English men have invented these [Christian] stories to amaze us and fear us out of our old customs, and bring us to stand in awe of them, that they might wipe us of our lands, and drive us into corners, to seek new ways of living and new places too? And be beholding to them for that which is our own, and was ours, before we knew them?" Yet members of the Natick community became Eliot's most effective missionaries. Attired in somber coats, cravats, and shoes and stockings, they went forth to preach the Puritan version of the gospel among the neighboring tribes, including the Nipmuck and Pawtucket. Largely because of their recruiting efforts, the experiment at Natick

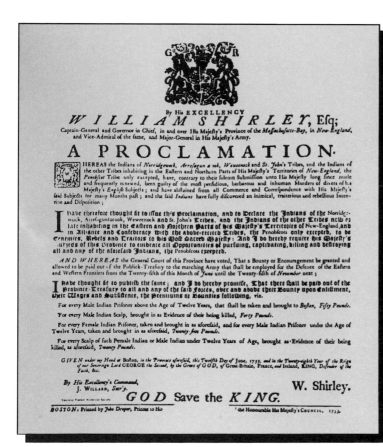

A public notice printed in 1755 proclaims all the Indians of eastern and northern New England except the Penobscot to be enemies of the British Crown and offers rewards for their capture or death. An adult male prisoner was worth £50, and his scalp £40. For females and children, £25 was offered for a captive, £20 for a scalp.

would be repeated again and again until there were 14 so-called praying towns with 2,200 Indian inhabitants on the mainland and between 1,800 and 2,600 on the islands of Martha's Vineyard and Nantucket.

The towns survived until 1675, when the Indian converts felt the full wrath of colonial resentment during the bloody uprising led by the Wampanoag sachem Metacomet, known to the English as King Philip. Even though most "praying" Indians remained neutral or allied themselves with the English, the colonists held them equally responsible for the war. Ten of the praying towns were destroyed during the fighting. Afterward, all those Indians who had not been killed, sold into slavery, or driven out of the region were confined to the four remaining praying towns. What had begun as sanctuaries now served as internment camps for the remnants of southern New England's entire native population.

The plight of the New England Indians was a harbinger of things to come for Native American communities all across the continent. In many respects, the praying towns were precursors to the system of reservations established by the United States government two centuries later. By that time, the vast majority of eastern tribes had been either exterminated or dispossessed and relocated beyond the Mississippi River, where vast new stretches of Indian land in the West were already being gobbled up or trespassed on by a relentless tide of white settlers. Soon there would be no more land beyond the reach of white settlement where Indians could seek refuge. America's indigenous peoples would become a small, peripheral minority group kept to the margins of white society by a complex of prejudices, economic dependency, and political powerlessness.

Like their early New England colonial predecessors, 19th-century American officials sought to restrict the Indians to particular tracts of land. And although the missionary fervor that shaped the praying towns was rarely present, the same impulse was at work—to make over the Indian in the image of the white man.

From the beginning, whites saw reservations as a way of "civilizing savages." The Indians, for their part, responded to the loss of their land and confinement to specific areas in various ways. Some resisted vigorously. Others viewed the existence of a reservation as a way of preserving their nation. With few options to choose from, many regarded the reservation as a bridge between their old, traditional world and the white world. As a result, most reservations became hybrid communities that allowed the residents to preserve central Indian values and a place of their own in the new order of things. Over and over again, Indian leaders repeated a common plea: Allow us to be ourselves. Often, however, these new communities were riven by disputing factions who either accepted or rejected white authority.

As in the praying towns, high-minded motives often animated the growth of the reservation system. Well-intentioned whites hoped to segregate and safeguard the Indians from aggressive settlers, isolate them from drink and other frontier evils, and "civilize" them for survival in white society. But at the heart of the reservation concept lay a less lofty intent. The Indians had the land and the white settlers wanted it—even if it meant forcing the removal and relocation of entire tribes.

Unlike the French and Spaniards, who came to the New World largely to exploit its wealth—the French as fur traders, the Spaniards as conquerors and treasure seekers—the English wanted to settle down and replace the native population. America's endless vistas were an irresistible magnet for dispossessed Englishmen who could never hope to gain property in a homeland cramped by the constraints of size and class structure. Scarcely a century after the first Pilgrims stepped ashore, more than one million English settlers were living in North America upon earth recently occupied and claimed by Indians.

The question of land claims was complicated by the sharply differing perspectives of the English and the Indians. Colonists thought of land as a commodity that could be bought and sold, cleared and cultivated, stripped of mineral wealth or of game animals. The Indians, by contrast, regarded it as a communal resource and viewed the custodianship of their traditional land base as a tribal birthright that often dated through origin stories to their beginnings as a people.

Each Native American group developed its own distinctive relationship with the land. "The old people came literally to love the soil,"

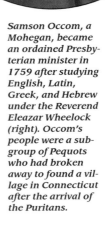

Samson Occom, a Mohegan, became an ordained Presbyterian minister in 1759 after studying English, Latin, Greek, and Hebrew under the Reverend Eleazar Wheelock (right). Occom's people were a subgroup of Pequots who had broken away to found a village in Connecticut after the arrival of the Puritans.

WILLIAM & MARY COLLEGE, WILLIAMSBURG, VA.

Chartered in 1693, the College of William and Mary taught Indian students from the early 1700s until 1776, when the onset of the American Revolution caused funding for the program to end. The Indians lived and studied in The Brafferton, the Georgian-style building at far left.

This wood engraving shows the Reverend Eleazar Wheelock instructing a class of Indian and white youths at Moor's Indian Charity School in Hanover, New Hampshire. Inspired by his success in tutoring Samson Occom, Wheelock founded the school in Lebanon, Connecticut, in 1754, later moving it to Hanover, where it formed the nucleus of Dartmouth College.

explained Luther Standing Bear, a Lakota Sioux who was a member of the first class at the Carlisle Indian Industrial School in Pennsylvania in 1879. "They sat on the ground with the feeling of being close to a mothering power. It was good for the skin to touch the earth, and the old people liked to remove their moccasins and walk with their bare feet on the sacred earth. The soil was soothing, strengthening, cleansing, and healing." Rivers, caves, trees, and other particular features of the landscape figured in the age-old stories that were passed down through the generations. "Every part of this soil is sacred in the estimation of my people," asserted Seathl, a 19th-century Suquamish Indian whose ancestral land bordered Puget Sound in the modern-day state of Washington. "Every hillside, every valley, every plain and grove, has been hallowed by some sad or happy event in days long vanished."

The Indians' perspective, however, meant little to land-hungry settlers. The early English colonists claimed land under the rubric of the so-called doctrine of discovery. This particular tenet of international law, as then recognized by the European powers, gave the discoverer of "wilderness" lands the right to acquire title through purchase or conquest. The Puritans who, in many instances, took over the cleared farmlands of Indians who had died of smallpox invoked their own doctrine of divine right, as articulated by Increase Mather, the 17th-century clergyman: "[The] Lord God Our Father hath given us for a rightful possession the lands of Heathen People amongst whom we live."

The English also argued that whites deserved the land because they could put it to better use. They regarded Indian practices as wasteful. Like other woodlands people, the New England tribes maintained, in addition to their villages and cultivated fields, a large preserve devoted to hunting and gathering. Colonists looked upon the latter as surplus. "Their land is spacious and void," said Robert Cushman, a Massachusetts Bay Colony clergyman, "and there are few and [they] do but run over the grass, as do also the foxes and wild beasts." To John Winthrop, the Cambridge-trained lawyer who later became governor of the colony, it was the settlers' divinely inspired duty to "take a land which none useth, and make use of it."

The idea of asserting sovereignty over lands in the New World was not a uniquely English phenomenon. It started with the papal bull of May 4, 1493, issued by Pope Alexander VI shortly after Columbus returned to Spain. In that document, the pope granted a deed to Spain's King Ferdinand and Queen Isabella for "all islands and mainlands found and to be found, discovered and to be discovered" beyond the Azores.

William Apess, an educated Pequot who fought for the United States in the War of 1812, became one of the first activists for Indian rights. A Methodist preacher, he worked among the Mashpee Indians and in 1833 petitioned the governor of Massachusetts to grant that tribe self-government.

For a solution to the problem of what to do with the Indians, the early colonists could look to recent English history. During the early part of the 17th century, Englishmen trying to colonize part of Scotland drove out many native Scots, some of whom settled in northern Ireland. The English suppressed native languages, banned tribal customs, and sent Scottish children away to English schools to be "civilized."

With these lessons in mind, the English colonists created little enclaves such as the praying towns. These reservations often consisted of land "reserved for" the tribe from much larger tracts ceded to the colonies by a treaty, sometimes after the Indians had been defeated in a war. A clear understanding of the transfer of property rights under such treaties sometimes eluded the Indians because of their different conception of land ownership and use as well as their leadership systems, in which no single individual had the authority to speak for all of the people. Now and again, the Indians resolved the problem temporarily by migrating to another area—an action that often brought them into conflict with other tribes already living there.

In addition to the praying towns, there was a burst of other reservation activity during the mid-17th century. The Massachusetts Bay Colony founded in southeastern Connecticut two reservations for remnants of the Pequots scattered by war with the whites. On Cape Cod during the 1660s, missionaries created a reservation at Mashpee for the surviving Wampanoags. In Virginia, meanwhile, officials in 1653 set aside areas for the Pamunkeys in York County and provided restricted areas for other Indians in Gloucester and Lancaster Counties. Other reservations took shape on Long Island and in North Carolina. It was not uncommon for the colonial governments to exact tribute from the Indians. Members of the Powhatan Confederacy, for example, were required to pay 20 beaver skins annually to the governor of Virginia.

The English were not alone among the colonial powers in their early experiments with reservation-like communities. In 1637, 14 years before the start of praying towns in the Massachusetts Bay Colony, French Jesuit missionaries in Canada established the first of eight Indian settlements in the Saint Lawrence Valley. In these so-called reserves, Hurons, Mohawks, and other seminomadic Indians were supposed to settle down and become easier targets for conversion to Catholicism. In sharp contrast with the praying towns of New England, however, the desire to acquire Indian land

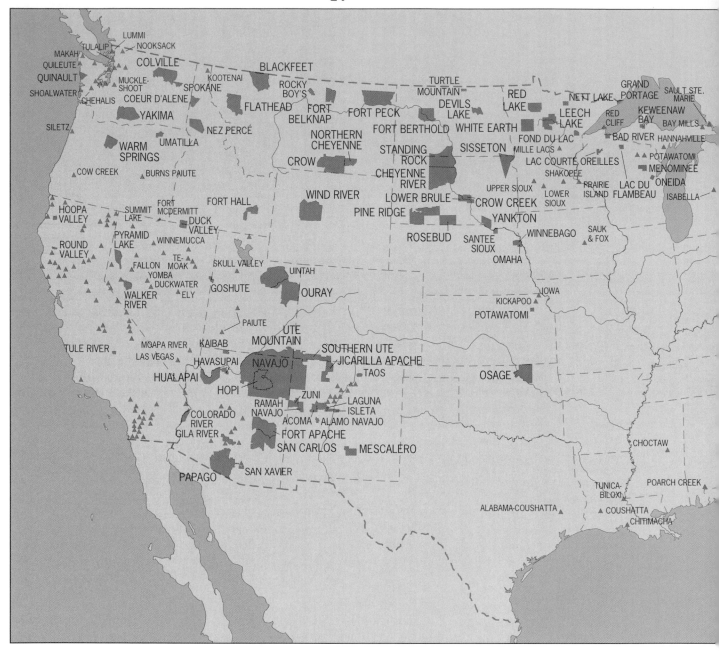

played no role here. France's interest in North America focused on the fur trade, an activity that transformed native economies but left the Indians in possession of their traditional areas. The Jesuits, on the other hand, were concerned only with saving souls. Indians who joined the reserves did so voluntarily. Inhabitants spoke their native tongues and lived in largely traditional housing. They chose their clothing from both cultures. Women continued to tend the corn while men went off to hunt and trade. After a brief period of close oversight by the priests, residents ruled themselves for all practical purposes, relying on traditional forms of government.

The most successful reserve, Caughnawaga (Kahnawake), attracted hundreds of Mohawks, Oneidas, and other members of the Iroquois confederacy from the Lake Champlain-Lake Ontario region. A Jesuit named

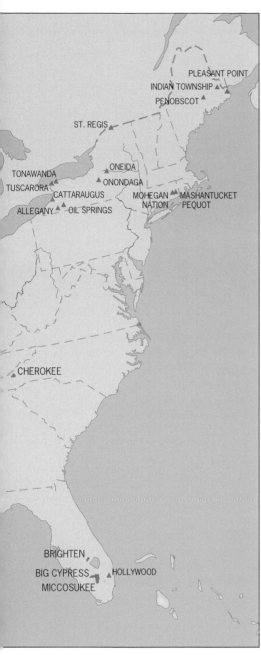

The map above shows the current locations of most of the more than 300 federally recognized Indian reservations within the continental United States. They range in size from tiny "rancherías" in California to the Navajo Reservation of more than 17 million acres in Arizona and neighboring states. Of the 1.2 million Indians who are members of the 319 federally recognized tribes, only about 437,000, or 22 percent, live on reservations.

Pierre Raffeix founded the settlement at Laprairie on the south bank of the Saint Lawrence River opposite the French village of Mont Réal (Montreal) in 1667. The tract fell within territory that the Iroquoians considered a part of their hunting grounds.

The first residents were seven Oneidas led by a man named Tonsahoten and his wife Catherine Gandeakteua. Both were Catholic converts and former members of other tribes—Tonsahoten was born a Huron and Gandeakteua an Erie—who had been captured by the Oneida and adopted. In 1669, at the urging of Father Raffeix, the couple built a house a few hundred yards from the French village at Laprairie. Other Indians joined them. From time to time, new members returned home to hunt or visit and recruited their families. Many Iroquois villages were riven by political and religious divisions, and Catholic converts were eager to migrate, especially to an area that promised prosperous trapping and trading. In 1674 the converted wife of a Mohawk war chief named Togouiroui succeeded in persuading her husband, who had been hostile to Christianity, to resettle at the reserve, and he brought along two large bands of his fellow Mohawks.

To the Jesuits, the greatest threats to the success of the reserve were polygamy and drunkenness, "the general perdition of all the Indian missions." Two trees symbolizing these evils stood at the entrance, and newcomers were supposed to "hang" their sinful inclinations on the branches, thus discarding them. But in 1676, after only nine years, the dangers of demon brandy sold in nearby French communities, together with the need for fresh land to accommodate its growing population of 300, forced the Indians and the Jesuits to move the reserve three miles upriver. The Jesuits named this new place Sault Saint Louis, after the nearby rapids, but the Indians continued to call it Caughnawaga after a village on the Mohawk River in their old homeland. The name stuck through three additional moves during the following 40 years, migrations that were aimed at gaining new land and getting farther away from the fleshpots of Montreal.

Religion at Caughnawaga was a hybrid of Roman Catholicism and Iroquois customs. Its special appeal to women may have stemmed from Catholicism's emphasis on the Virgin Mary and the Iroquois matrilineal tradition, in which descent was traced through the mother. The French priests cultivated this inclination by organizing female societies and encouraging adolescent girls to vow lifelong chastity. On occasion some women went beyond what the Jesuits asked. During the late 1670s, before women of the reserve were permitted to take religious orders and become nuns, a small group displayed a remarkable outpouring of spirituality.

They performed a number of acts of self-mortification that seemed to combine Catholic and Indian traditions. Some of their deeds, such as plunging themselves into the freezing river, were familiar acts of penitence. Other physical torments that they inflicted on themselves, such as inserting red-hot coals between their toes, seemed to be taken from Iroquois methods of ritual torture.

One of the leading participants in the spiritual ferment was a young Mohawk named Kateri Tekakwitha. Sickly, partially blind, and fiercely devout, she had been baptized at age 20 by Jesuits in her native village of Ossernenon in New York's Mohawk Valley. Hounded by traditionalists, she fled to Caughnawaga, where, according to a contemporary account, she renounced everyday "amusements" and devoted herself to "prayers, toil, [and] spiritual conversation." She was the first Iroquois to become a nun and, after dying from disease while still in her twenties, the object of much veneration. Her fellow penitents prayed at her grave, and pilgrims from all over the region—French as well as Indian—came to experience the miraculous cures that reportedly occurred there. Revered as the Lily of the Mohawks, she was accorded beatification—the second step toward sainthood—by the Vatican three centuries later.

Over the years, the Jesuit jurisdiction at Caughnawaga faded, but Catholicism, and the settlement itself, thrived. By 1730 Caughnawaga had attracted a population of 1,000, composed mostly of Mohawks. A flourishing mix of cultures, where young men sometimes wore their warrior garb to Mass, the reserve was the most populous Indian settlement in New France and one of the largest in eastern North America.

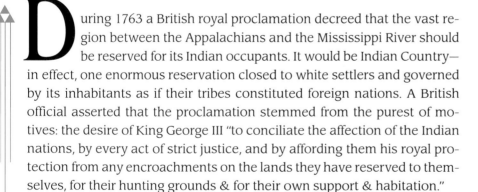

During 1763 a British royal proclamation decreed that the vast region between the Appalachians and the Mississippi River should be reserved for its Indian occupants. It would be Indian Country— in effect, one enormous reservation closed to white settlers and governed by its inhabitants as if their tribes constituted foreign nations. A British official asserted that the proclamation stemmed from the purest of motives: the desire of King George III "to conciliate the affection of the Indian nations, by every act of strict justice, and by affording them his royal protection from any encroachments on the lands they have reserved to themselves, for their hunting grounds & for their own support & habitation."

But few officials regarded this Appalachian line of separation as a permanent barrier. Its essential purposes were to increase the power of the imperial government and to block the westward expansion of the American colonies. The proclamation provided procedures under which the barrier could be nudged westward. Each tribe was considered to be an independent nation; treaties allowing cessions of land could be negotiated in formal councils between tribal leaders and representatives of the Crown. Over the next decade, a series of such treaties launched the relentless march of the boundary westward with its consequent reduction of the immense reserve known as Indian Country.

Because it frustrated western expansion of the colonies, the Proclamation of 1763 was one of the issues that helped spark the American Revolution. But in the end, the victorious rebels themselves embraced the principle of a separate Indian Country. They too considered the boundary line subject to change. After all, Indians still controlled some 90 percent of the land transferred to the colonists by Great Britain after the Revolution. (This transfer was made in 1783 through the Treaty of Paris, a document that said not a word about the Indians.) The concept of maintaining a separate Indian Country while shrinking it with land cessions appeared in the Northwest Ordinance of 1787. Congress pledged "utmost good faith shall always be observed towards the Indians" and vowed never to take their lands and property "without their consent." At the same time, the act provided for the creation of new states between the Ohio and Mississippi Rivers, thus anticipating the erosion of Indian Country.

Treaties negotiated between the fledgling United States and the Miami, Shawnee, Delaware, and other tribes moved the frontier westward through Ohio and established boundaries between Indian and white settlements. But settler aggression and Indian retaliation continued as the tribes refused to yield more land. In the spring of 1794, an overwhelming force of regular troops and volunteers led by General Anthony Wayne defeated the Indians at Fallen Timbers. The following year, delegations of Delawares, Ottawas, Miamis, Ojibwas, Potawatomis, Shawnees, and Hurons gathered at a peace conference at Fort Greenville in the Indiana Territory. Bargaining as forcefully as they could, the Indian leaders accepted a tactical retreat in exchange for annuities and, more important, United States recognition of a new white-Indian border.

The Greenville treaty and others, such as those made by the English colonists, were based on an assumption that bedevils the courts to this day. In theory, the federal government recognized the sovereignty of Indian tribes and negotiated treaties with them—to be ratified by the Senate in accordance with rules established by the U.S. Constitution—as if they were

The photographs on the following pages show the variety of lands reserved by Indians or set aside as Indian reservations. From swamp to desert, grassland to mountain, they vary not only in terrain but also in their proximity to the residents' original homelands. Ancestors of the Seminoles living on the Miccosukee Indian Reservation, which includes part of Florida's Everglades (right), came from lands that are now South Carolina and Georgia.

A GALLERY OF RESERVATION LANDS

foreign nations. In reality, government negotiators frequently employed threats, military force, bribery, or guile to win the signatures of Indian leaders who frequently did not fully understand the English-language documents and were often unaware that they were signing away their land. The great 19th-century Sauk war leader Black Hawk spoke for many when he said, "I touched the goose quill to the treaty, not knowing that, by that act, I consented to give away my village." Yet the fact that U.S. negotiators accepted the tribes as legal equals at the time allows modern Indians to legitimately claim that their treaty-recognized domains are a kind of sovereign state and thus deserving of special prerogatives under American law—an argument that remains at the heart of Indian political life today.

While the federal government cut into Indian Country in the decades following the Revolutionary War, tribes that had survived within the newly established states saw their ancestral lands shrivel. The state of Massachusetts forced the Penobscot of present-day Maine to sell off so much land that they were finally confined to Indian Island at Old Town and other islands of the Penobscot River. In New York State, fighting during the Revolution had splintered the once powerful Iroquois confederacy. Afterward, the Mohawk war chief Joseph Brant, who had sided with the British, led more than 1,800 Iroquois into Canada to settle on a large British-provided reserve along the Grand River. Those Senecas, Onondagas, and Oneidas who remained sold much of their territory to the state of New York or to private entrepreneurs but reserved some of the best land for themselves. Annuities from the land sales helped ease the transition from hunting to farming on their self-chosen sites.

A far-reaching new proposal for the removal and resettlement of Indians came from President Thomas Jefferson in 1803. Jefferson had just completed the purchase from France of a region so vast, stretching from the Gulf of Mexico to Canada and from the Mississippi to the Rocky Mountains, that it instantly doubled the size of the United States. Seeing in this Louisiana Purchase the opportunity to create a new Indian Country, he suggested that tribes living in the old Indian Country east of the Mississippi be encouraged to exchange their lands for territory west of the river. At Jefferson's request, Congress authorized the president to seek treaties that would provide for voluntary removal.

A mixture of motives underlay Jefferson's idea. Unlike many Anglo-Americans, he considered Indians "to be in body and mind equal to the whiteman" and harbored a genuine concern for their welfare. He believed

PINE RIDGE RESERVATION. *These rolling plains of southwestern South Dakota once supported vast herds of buffalo. The reservation represents a fraction of the great homeland set aside for the Lakota Sioux in 1868 but reclaimed nine years later by the United States after the discovery of gold in the sacred Black Hills adjoining the reservation.*

their survival depended on their settling down on family farms and practicing European-style agriculture. For the first time since the praying towns, reservations were to have a consciously moral and educational purpose. They were to be not only places of refuge but also places where "progress" could take place. Removal to the West would provide protection from whites and time to prepare for assimilation. At the same time, Jefferson fully realized that such a transformation would benefit white settlers by enabling Indians "to live on much smaller portions of land." He saw no contradiction in working for Indian advancement while suggesting ways to reduce their landholdings: "While they are learning to do better on less land, our increasing numbers will be calling for more land, and thus a coincidence of interests [will occur]."

Another Jefferson policy illustrated both his benevolence toward the Indians and his willingness to relieve them of their land. Starting in 1796, the federal government had constructed a number of trading posts in an attempt to regulate commerce on the frontier. The posts exchanged firearms and ammunition, pots and pans, blankets, and other manufactured goods for animal hides brought in by the Indians. Jefferson recommended building more trading houses in the hope that items of domestic comfort might induce the Indians to abandon their traditional ways and settle into a life of farming. He also directed the federal agents to encourage Indians to run up debts. "We observe that when these debts get beyond what the individuals can pay," the president wrote, "they become willing to lop them off by a cession of lands."

The policy of removal—at first voluntary, later forced—launched a chaotic era that would culminate in wholesale resettlement. Between 1789 and 1868, no fewer than 76 treaties calling for emigration westward would be concluded, and nearly 100 more would redraw existing Indian boundaries. Removal accelerated the migration of tribes such as the Delaware, who under white pressure made eight major moves from their original homeland on lands that are today part of the states of New York, New Jersey, Pennsylvania, and Delaware. By 1829 the Delaware were in present-day eastern Kansas, and they would eventually wind up in several states including Oklahoma. In all, more than 100,000 people from 28 tribes had been deported west of the Mississippi by mid-century.

At first, much of the removal took place in the still unsettled territory east of the Mississippi. Perhaps the official most skillful at separating Indians from their ancestral land in the Old Northwest was William Henry

PYRAMID LAKE INDIAN RESERVATION. *The land encompassed by this reservation in Nevada has been home to the Northern Paiute for centuries. The lake is a remnant of a vast prehistoric inland sea that once covered the entire Great Basin. The Paiute keep it well stocked with trout as part of a flourishing tourist business they developed.*

Harrison, the governor of the Indiana Territory, who later became ninth president of the United States. Between 1800 and 1812, Harrison negotiated 15 treaties. The treaties relegated the Delaware, Potawatomi, Miami, and other tribes to small local reservations and, at an average cost of about a penny an acre, yielded title to much of the American Middle West. Harrison then led troops in decisive victories over the Shawnee and other Indians during the War of 1812 that destroyed the Indians' military power.

The exodus beyond the Mississippi began as a trickle. Jefferson persuaded some 2,000 Cherokees to move from Tennessee to what is now Arkansas. Many Cherokees believed that the migration would give them a better chance to preserve their communities and maintain their tribal way of life. These newcomers soon encountered one of the ironies of the removal policy: Other Indians already occupied these prairies and plains and did not welcome intruders. Comanches, Pawnees, and Osages raided the livestock and farms of the Cherokees. The Cherokees had to call on their warrior tradition in order to survive in the West.

The migrant Cherokees' greatest challenge came from the Osage, who had lived in the region for centuries. The principal Osage war chief was White Hair, a striking man who wore as a charm a white wig he had taken from an American officer, along with a general's uniform and stovepipe hat presented to him by President Jefferson at the White House in 1804. White Hair's warriors made life miserable for the Cherokees in Arkansas, killing hundreds in the first wave of immigrants and bringing down the wrath of the federal government. In 1808 the Osage were forced to cede northern Arkansas and most of Missouri in the first of a series of treaties through which the government sought to make room for Cherokees and other eastern immigrants. In 1817 the Cherokees avenged their earlier losses by destroying an Osage village while the Osage men were away hunting buffalo. Subsequent treaties from 1818 to 1825 took away Osage lands in northern Oklahoma and southern Kansas, confining the tribe to a small reservation between the modern states. Other resident tribes, including the Oto and Kansa, also had to accept reduced domains in order to accommodate Indian immigrants.

A few other tribes followed the Cherokees westward. The Kickapoo, an Algonquian-speaking people originally from the Great Lakes region, agreed in 1819 to exchange their lands on the Wabash and Illinois Rivers for a tract in Missouri, from which they would later be removed westward again. That same year, hoping to persuade the Kickapoo and others to

NORTHERN CHEYENNE INDIAN RESERVA-TION. The U.S. government granted the Northern Cheyenne land in southern Montana, a part of their traditional range, in 1884. Prior to that, the Northern Cheyenne had been forcibly settled far from their homeland in the Indian Territory (modern-day Oklahoma) after the last of the Plains wars.

accept white civilization, Congress appropriated $10,000 annually to teach them to read, write, and farm the white man's way. In recommending the appropriation, a congressional committee wrote a popular prescription for taming "wild" Indians: "Put into the hands of their children the primer and the hoe, and they will naturally, in time, take hold of the plough. . .and they will grow up in habits of morality and industry."

Such inducements had little effect. So few tribes had been removed by 1825 that President James Monroe suggested a drastic measure. He proposed moving all eastern tribes at government expense to a permanent reserve set aside for the purpose. Because of the rapid advance of the frontier, he specified a new Indian Country farther west—beyond the Arkansas Territory and Missouri, which was now a state, and between the Platte River to the north and the Red River to the south. The Indian Territory, as it came to be known, consisted of present-day Oklahoma and parts of Nebraska and Kansas. The area had been dubbed the Great American Desert by one explorer, and there was some feeling that it might not be fit for white settlement anyway. President Monroe suggested that the Indian Territory might even have its own government. The most vocal proponent of a permanent Indian Country was Isaac McCoy, a self-educated Baptist minister who preached to the Miami, Potawatomi, and Ottawa in the Indiana and Michigan Territories. Twice, pressure from settlers had forced McCoy to relocate his mission, and he was convinced that the only way to save the Indians was to allow them a sanctuary where they could develop unhampered by white aggression. But the idea gathered little enthusiasm in Congress or among most Indians, who saw it as a dire threat to tribal nationalism and their way of life.

By 1828, when Andrew Jackson was elected president, additional northern tribes had migrated, but enormous numbers of Indians remained in the Southeast. More than 70,000 Cherokees, Chickasaws, Choctaws, Creeks, and Seminoles were still resident there. The Americans had labeled these peoples the Five Civilized Tribes because so many of them had adopted the ways of the white man or had married whites. They wore the white man's garb, lived in houses, farmed neatly tilled fields, and raised livestock; their children attended missionary schools. Some of the wealthy ones even owned black slaves. The Cherokees developed their own constitution based on that of the United States and published a newspaper written in their own alphabet. Their principal chief, John Ross, elected the same year as Jackson, had served in a Cherokee regiment under Jackson during

NAVAJO INDIAN RESERVATION. The largest in the United States, the Navajo Reservation takes up a large portion of northeastern Arizona, as well as smaller bits of Utah, Colorado, and New Mexico, and features some of the world's most dramatic landscapes, such as this section of Monument Valley. Some Navajos still live in hogans similar to those pictured in the foreground.

the Creek War of 1813-1814. That the Cherokees more than met Jefferson's criteria for inclusion in white society mattered little to Andrew Jackson.

Jackson was a Tennessean and an old Indian fighter whom the Indians called Sharp Knife. Unlike Jefferson, he believed the southeastern Indians possessed "neither the intelligence, the industry, the moral habits, nor the desire of improvement" to live among whites. He sympathized with the southern whites who coveted Indian land in Georgia, Alabama, Mississippi, and Florida. The tribes already had ceded much territory in an attempt to appease the whites. But the few thousand Cherokees and Choctaws who had moved west voluntarily were not nearly enough to suit the settlers, who were exerting intense pressure through their state governments to get rid of the Indians.

Under Jackson, removal became official government policy. He refused to intervene when Georgia, Alabama, and Mississippi passed laws that tried to abolish tribal governments and violate Indian rights, such as the measure that enabled Georgians to blatantly confiscate Cherokee land after the discovery of gold in the state in 1829. Lawyers representing the Cherokees appealed the case to the U.S. Supreme Court to establish the unconstitutionality of Georgia's actions. But the Indians' legal victory in *Worcester v. Georgia* rang hollow when President Jackson failed to enforce the Court's decision. He pushed through Congress, meanwhile, the notorious Indian Removal Act of 1830. Although the measure, which narrowly passed, made no mention of forcible relocation, there was never any question of how Jackson would proceed. Under his direction, U.S. commissioners coerced each of the Five Civilized Tribes into signing treaties that traded their ancestral lands for the promise of annuity payments and lesser tracts in the southern part of the Indian Territory.

These treaties triggered more than a decade of strife and tragedy. Only the Chickasaws of northern Mississippi and northwestern Alabama experienced a relatively smooth passage to their new home. After selling their eastern lands for a substantial sum and with good management from their tribal leaders and a shorter distance to travel, they journeyed west in good order. At the opposite extreme, the Seminoles began a seven-year guerrilla war against the army in the swamps of Florida before succumbing in 1842.

Extraordinary suffering marked the exodus of the other tribes as they made their way westward by foot, wagon, horseback, and riverboat. The army herded the Choctaws of southern Mississippi and southwestern Alabama through harsh winter cold and snow, amid epidemics of cholera

and smallpox, all of which claimed the lives of at least 6,000 of the 40,000 migrants. Of the 15,000 Creeks of western Georgia and Alabama who were forced westward, many of them in chains, half may have perished.

No tribe suffered more than the Cherokees of northwest Georgia, eastern Tennessee, and eastern Alabama, who lost at least 4,000 members to exposure, exhaustion, and disease. This tribe, which split into bitter factions over the question of relocation, was rounded up and interned in concentration camps before being sent on a 1,000-mile journey the Cherokees called Nunna daul Tsunyi, or Trail of Tears, a poignant term that came to be applied to the ordeal of every tribe forced westward by Jackson's cruel policy.

Jackson paid less attention to the tribes still remaining in the Northwest Territory, and these smaller groups were transplanted at a slower pace. Shawnees, Ottawas, and a group of Senecas who had earlier migrated to northern Ohio moved with some dispatch, trading tracts of land for equivalent territory in the West. The Potawatomi, in contrast, lost their land piecemeal over a long period of time. Between 1789 and 1837, the tribe signed 39 treaties that slowly whittled away their homelands. The last few of these treaties ceded some 120 miniature reserves where scattered bands lived in Michigan, Indiana, and Illinois. Hundreds of these Indians eventually drifted northward into Canada and established communities along the eastern shore of Lake Huron rather than move westward with the bulk of their brethren.

The Potawatomi's former neighbors, the Miami, held out even longer. Leaders of this once powerful confederacy clung to a 500,000-acre reserve on the south side of the Wabash River until 1840, when they traded it for trans-Mississippi land and were given five years to move. The Miami were still in Indiana in 1846—four years after all but 300 of the Seminole fugitives had been shipped west. The army escorted the Miami away, but only 323 arrived at their new reservation in Kansas. About half the tribe had evaded the troops. They, and others who had gone west, later made their way back to Indiana, where more than a century later, some 700 of them remained. Another tribe, the Menominee, refused to vacate their ancestral land in Wisconsin and eventually persuaded state authorities to provide them with a reservation on the Wolf River.

One group of northern Indians staged a rebellion against removal. The confederation of the Sauk and the Fox had formally ceded their extensive holdings in Illinois and Wisconsin in the treaty wrought by William Henry

Harrison in 1804. Under the terms of that agreement, the Indians were allowed to remain in Illinois until white settlement caught up with them; then they were supposed to cross the Mississippi into Iowa. In 1831 most of them left. The following year, however, a dissident faction under the leadership of Black Hawk insisted on returning to Illinois for the planting season. His 500 warriors defended their homeland valiantly until U.S. Army troops and militia volunteers defeated them in the so-called Black Hawk War. The Sauk and Fox settled on a 400-square-mile reservation along the Iowa River but a decade later, crowded by white settlers, sold their remaining lands in Iowa and relocated in the northern Indian Territory.

By the mid-1840s, some 100,000 members of more than a dozen eastern tribes occupied reservations in the Indian Territory. Only about 23,000 Indians remained east of the Mississippi. The northern portion of the Indian Territory—present-day Kansas and Nebraska—consisted of a crazy-quilt pattern of tribes and languages. The reservations of such Northwest Territory peoples as the Kickapoo, Ottawa, and Shawnee abutted the lands of longtime residents of the eastern Great Plains—the Pawnee, Missouri, and Osage. Unlike later reservations, these tracts were typically large, with loosely defined boundaries, and subject to practically no interference from the federal government.

The southern portion—Oklahoma—accommodated some 60,000 members of the Five Civilized Tribes. Having endured such trauma en route to their new lands, they worked hard to rebuild their lives, establishing farms and cotton plantations in the fertile river valleys, building schools and churches, running gristmills, and operating prosperous trading posts. Observing their struggles but not comprehending their significance, the U.S. commissioner of Indian affairs, Orlando Brown, credited the ordeal of removal for the "light of Christianity and general knowledge dawning upon their moral and intellectual darkness."

The base upon which the Indian Territory was founded—the concept of a permanent boundary separating Native Americans from whites—was soon threatened. During the late 1840s, acquisitions of more than one million square miles by the United States pushed the frontier from the Mississippi River all the way to the Pacific Ocean. Texas was annexed in 1845 and the Oregon country acquired by treaty with Great Britain in 1846; in 1848, at the conclusion of the Mexican War, came the vast lands that would become the states of New Mexico, California, Arizona, and Utah. The Indian Territory was almost immediately slashed by westward trails of settlers, adventurers, and, within two decades, passengers on the

Signed by President Martin Van Buren in 1838, this document conveyed to the Cherokee two tracts of land totaling 14 million acres in Arkansas. The United States reserved the right to build roads and forts throughout the territory.

newly built transcontinental railroads fulfilling what came to be known as America's doctrine of Manifest Destiny.

Once again the Indians had a massive white problem. The federal government began to chip off large chunks of the Indian Territory that the government itself had created. The northern portion disappeared as Congress partitioned that region into the Kansas and Nebraska Territories. The dozen tribes living there, including the Sauk and Fox, Omaha, Kickapoo, and Delaware, were coerced into ceding most of their lands and accepting smaller reservations. And in the southern portion, as punishment because some factions had collaborated with the Confederates during the Civil War, the Five Civilized Tribes had to surrender the western half of their territory to accommodate other Indian groups being relocated to make way for whites. "I have listened to a great many talks from our Great Father," complained the Creek chief Speckled Snake, "but they always began and ended in this—Get a little farther; you are too near me."

Scores of other tribes west of the Indian Territory experienced tumult because of the United States' expansion to the Pacific. Perhaps as many as 300,000 Indians lived in the newly acquired region. A diverse lot, they included nomads such as the Comanche and Apache of the Southwest, the agricultural, house-dwelling Pueblo Indians of New Mexico, and the countless small hunter-gatherer tribes of California. Now for the first time, the buffalo hunters on the northern Great Plains began coming into increasing contact with large numbers of white Americans.

United States officials and tribal leaders often had a common purpose—a stable border between their respective communities. The federal solution officially set forth in 1850 had a familiar ring. Luke Lea, the commissioner of Indian affairs, spelled out the plan: "There should be assigned to each tribe, for a permanent home, a country adapted to agriculture, of limited extent and well-defined boundaries; within which all, with occasional exceptions, should be compelled constantly to remain until such

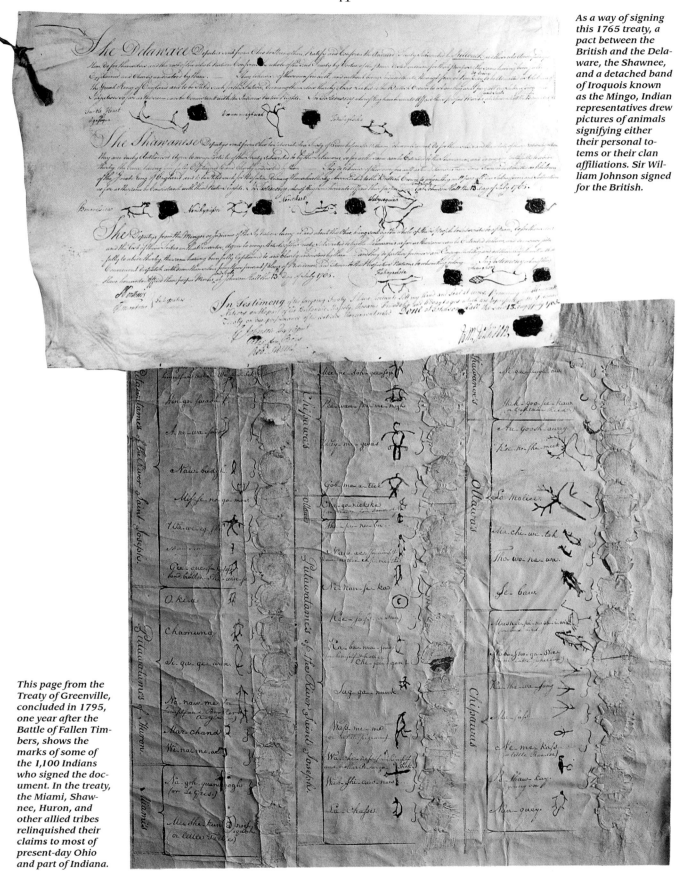

As a way of signing this 1765 treaty, a pact between the British and the Delaware, the Shawnee, and a detached band of Iroquois known as the Mingo, Indian representatives drew pictures of animals signifying either their personal totems or their clan affiliations. Sir William Johnson signed for the British.

This page from the Treaty of Greenville, concluded in 1795, one year after the Battle of Fallen Timbers, shows the marks of some of the 1,100 Indians who signed the document. In the treaty, the Miami, Shawnee, Huron, and other allied tribes relinquished their claims to most of present-day Ohio and part of Indiana.

These picture signatures of Abenaki leaders and their allies were affixed to a letter the Indians wrote to the governor of the Massachusetts Bay Colony on July 27, 1721. The names of the various Indian groups were written in French, bespeaking the Abenaki's long history of diplomatic relations with New France.

time as their general improvement and good conduct may supersede the necessity of such restrictions."

The new reservation policy culminated the process that had begun back in 1651 with the praying towns of colonial New England. The federal government would help the Indians build homes and, in Lea's words, "secure to them the means and facilities of education, intellectual, moral, and religious." Reservations were to be closed to all whites except for a staff supervised by a resident federal agent. Indian children were to be educated in schools that taught manual skills. There was to be enough land to allow some hunting, and food, clothing, and other rations would be distributed as necessary. But the aim was to make the inhabitants into full-time farmers or stockmen.

Although sometimes cloaked in fresh phrases and intellectual finery, the rationale for the new reservation policy differed little from that of the praying towns. Segregation would protect the Indians from white settlers and other Indians. Reservations were the only alternative to extinction, or so the thinking went, because they would allow the Indians time to adopt farming, Christianity, the English language, and other ways of the white man. Once the Indians had accomplished all this and given up their tribal identities, they would be ready for "ultimate incorporation into the great body of our citizen population," as Commissioner Lea put it. The reservation would vanish, allowing sale of surplus land to whites. The immediate goal, however, was to get the Indians out of the way. Treaties for the purpose of buying up land and creating the new reservations became the principal instrument of U.S. policy in the West—and the source of repeated violence and warfare over the next three decades.

One of the first tests of the concept came in newly annexed Texas. In 1854 federal agents established two reservations near the Brazos River on land grudgingly provided by the state. On one location, Tonkawas, Wichitas, and remnants of the once flourishing Caddos built thatch-roofed shelters and planted corn as they had for centuries. On the other reservation, some 400 Comanches showed little interest in the settled life. Raids in the region by nonreservation Indians stirred up white settlers. These settlers, making no distinction between peaceful and warring Indians, retaliated

Ojibwa clan leaders indicated their agreement with one another by drawing lines connecting the hearts and eyes of their clan totems. In the letter to which these drawings were attached, the Ojibwa were demanding that the U.S. government restore their lands.

Osage Indians angered by the coming of the railroad across their lands in the Kansas Territory sent this drawing along with a formal protest to the federal government in the mid-1800s. The locomotive, labeled No Soul, is crushing an Osage beneath its wheels.

against the reservations. The attacks mounted so alarmingly that in 1859 the federal government shut down the reservations and moved the 1,500 residents across the Red River to a new reservation in the Indian Territory carved from land leased from the Chickasaw.

The reservation plan also ran into problems in California. In 1852, by which time the state's large Indian population had been decimated by disease and overwhelmed by the gold rush, federal commissioners concluded the last of 18 treaties. Each treaty called for a reservation so big that the aggregate territory would amount to about 7.5 percent of the state's dominion, including prime agricultural and mineral lands. But outraged whites generated enough pressure to help defeat the treaties in Congress.

Federal agents then improvised, establishing seven small reservations on federal lands, beginning in 1853. Intended as secular versions of the old Spanish missions, these reservations were situated around military outposts designed to protect the residents from whites. The sites consisted of no more than 25,000 acres and seldom were suitable for the farming that was supposed to sustain the Indians. The population of these reservations reached a peak of 10,000 in 1857—about one-fifth of the surviving Indians in the state—and then went into decline. Residents on these parcels, unlike those on most reservations, had no legal claim to the land and could be relocated at any time. They were defrauded by agents, attacked by settlers who stole parts of the federal land, and demoralized by having to live with mixed populations drawn indiscriminately from different tribal groups. These and other problems forced the closing of all but three of the reservations during the following decade.

In the Pacific Northwest and the Spanish Southwest, Indians violently resisted reservations. Many tribes in the territories of Oregon and Washington—most notably the Yakima—had to be defeated militarily during the 1850s before settling on small tracts reserved from their former domains. The Navajo of New Mexico and Arizona held out even longer. Eventually the Navajo were subdued and forced to join some Mescalero Apaches on a barren reservation called Bosque Redondo in eastern New Mexico. To get there, some 8,000 Navajos endured what became seared in tribal memory as the Long Walk, a 300-mile ordeal over mountain and desert.

What they found at the end was 40 square miles of land so drought-stricken and unproductive that raising corn and other crops proved nearly impossible. After four years of hunger and disease that claimed perhaps one-fourth of the Indian community, officials tried to persuade the Navajos to move to the Indian Territory in Oklahoma. The Navajos refused and finally won approval to return to their native Arizona, where they rebuilt their lives on a reservation set aside on a section of their former domain.

The Great Plains were the arena for the most protracted Indian resistance. Because of the military prowess of the Sioux, Cheyenne, Comanche, and other Plains tribes, government officials moved slowly in implementing their new policy. A start was made in 1851 at Fort Laramie in the Wyoming Territory, where a gathering of nearly 10,000 members of eight tribes agreed to stop harassing westward-bound settlers and stick to defined hunting territories in return for annuities of food, livestock, and merchandise and promises of protection against white encroachers. After repeated warfare sparked by the trespassing of white emigrants heading west, these loosely defined territories would evolve, in greatly shrunken form, into reservations during the next two decades. Under a second Treaty of Fort Laramie, signed in 1868, the Great Sioux Reservation was established in the western half of present-day South Dakota.

The crucial agreement on the southern Plains was the Treaty of Medicine Lodge concluded in 1867. The Southern Cheyenne, Arapaho, Comanche, Kiowa, and Kiowa Apache signed papers committing them to the reservation policy. In return for surrendering their claims to immense areas of land, they accepted two reservations of about 5,500 square miles each in the western part of the Indian Territory, the area forfeited by the Five Civilized Tribes after the Civil War. Soon, after additional reshuffling, some 30 different Indian groups had been stuffed into a reduced Indian Territory that approximated the borders of present-day Oklahoma.

The agreements assigning reservations to the Plains tribes were among the last such treaties negotiated by the federal government. In 1871 Congress approved a law formally ending what Andrew Jackson, the architect of forced removal, had called the "farce of treating with Indian tribes." Exactly 374 treaties had been signed, many of them for the purpose of establishing reservations, and as Jackson had suggested, the process had long since degenerated into a hollow formality. The takeover of Indian lands was complete for now, and it would be up to the army to finish the work by corralling the remaining bands of recalcitrants. A decade later, when that roundup was virtually over, some 360,000 Indians were contained on 441 federal reservations in 21 states and territories. In recalling the sad history of his people, an old Lakota Sioux warrior summed up three centuries of relations with the white man: "They made us many promises, more than I can remember," the man said. "But they kept but one. They promised to take our land, and they took it." ✦

INDIANS ON DISPLAY

At the Saint Louis World's Fair of 1904, millions of visitors came to see the Indians. On a hillside at the fair's site, an assemblage of Native Americans from many tribes and regions lived in a conglomeration of artificial villages, staging demonstrations and performing rituals for the public.

The fair celebrated the centennial of the Louisiana Purchase—a year late because of organizing delays. The Native Americans were part of what W. J. McGee, chief of the fair's anthropology presentations, called a "comprehensive exhibit of the primitive peoples of the globe" and as such were joined on display by African pygmies, Patagonian "giants," and Ainus from Japan—all selected, McGee said, for being "least removed from the subhuman form." But if the Native Americans took umbrage at this official attitude, or were even aware of it, no record of their reaction has come to light.

Many of the Indians were eager to earn money selling their handiwork, such as painted buckskin, pipes, beadwork, and baskets. Proud Indian youths demonstrated their expertise at wagon making while whites watched. And the great Chiricahua Apache war chief Geronimo was not at all embarrassed to sell his autograph for a dime each to souvenir seekers who clearly were delighted to buy it.

The sham villages and Indian performances were convincing to varying degrees. A pueblo that rose 60 feet above the main fairgrounds was an authentic-looking copy of an Arizona adobe community. But the perspiration of fur-clad Eskimos sweltering in the Missouri summer heat belied the "Arctic" effects of white scenery. Still, the *Saint Louis Post-Dispatch* summed up the Indian exhibits as the "Real Thing in the TeePee Line."

It is not known that any of the Indians were compelled to attend the fair, although apparently the Osages complained considerably about their living conditions there. They "were extremely hard to please," noted one official publication, probably because they "lived too well at home." (As members of a small tribe exceedingly wealthy in oil and gas royalties, land, and an interest-bearing account of some $8 million, many Osages resided in stone houses and were said to employ whites as farm hands and domestic servants.) Disgruntled as they might have been, however, they still performed their ancient ceremonial dances every day.

Before the seven-month-long exposition ended, the Native American exhibits attracted three million people, so many that officials added an extra stop to the little railway that shuttled visitors around the fairgrounds. Called Indian Station, the stop was at the top of the hill, next to the Indian School, where students from across the country showed off their academic and craft skills. The students, McGee said, were "savages, made, by American methods, into civilized workers."

Native Americans themselves flocked to the fair by the hundreds; it was said that at one time members of 67 different tribes were on the premises. It is unlikely that they viewed the students as reshaped savages. As would any concerned parents, most Indian visitors headed first for the school to see what the future held for their own children.

Some of its 150 students line the front steps of the government Indian School—the grandest and most modern structure in the fair's Native American section. Within, children from kindergarten up were taught in front of visitors. Each afternoon a brass band of Indian boys gave a concert in front of the building

On April 30, 1904, the opening day of the
world's fair, a "cavalcade of strange animals
and stranger peoples" marches through the
grounds (above). The official history said
the parade included the "semicivilized, bar-
baric, and savage"—categories apparently
intended to encompass Indians.

Apache chief Geronimo (right) was loath to
leave internment in Oklahoma to attend the
fair. But once there, he was happy to make
"plenty of money—more than I had ever
owned before"—by selling his pictures and
autograph. He was amazed by a magician
who seemed to run a sword through a woman
without injuring her. And he rode on a Ferris
wheel: "I was scared," the old warrior said.

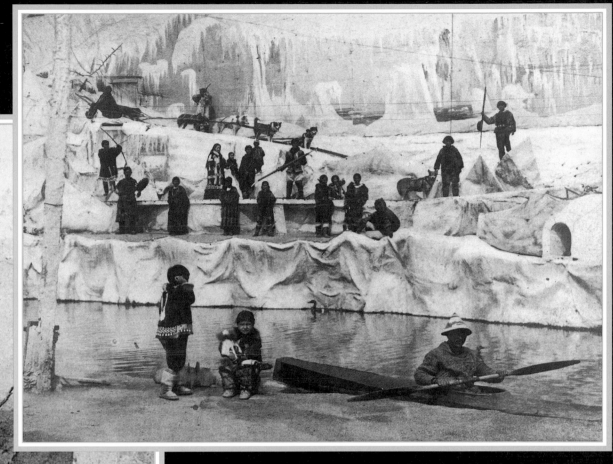

In a setting (above) that the official photo album considered "enough like nature to prompt at least the suggestion of coolness," an Alaskan Aleut maneuvers his boat, called a bidarka, to demonstrate how he would chase a sea otter if at home in the wild. In the background, a team of dogs is hitched to the kind of sled on which they pulled visitors through the Far North exhibits. An igloo made of artificial ice is at right.

Before a painted mountain, Eskimos loll in an ersatz Arctic village. The white editors of the official fair photo album said the log house at right represented "Esquimau progress toward civilization," especially as an "improvement on the ice home of the primitive Esquimau." Visitors taking the sled ride saw a "striking imitation of the northern aurora" and a "realistic combat between the sturdy Esquimaux and polar bear."

Jane Me-gay-zeuce Walters, an Ojibwa woman from the Great Lakes region, beads a traditional Anishinabe floral design into what will be a belt or a sash. Ojibwa women were considered the most expert bead workers at the exposition. They were also skilled at making baskets, yarn bags such as the one before Jane Walters, and rush mats like the one she is sitting on.

Five prominent Ojibwas gather before a traditional bark-covered wigwam. In the center holding the peace pipe is Lowering Feather, 86-year-old head chief of the Minnesota Ojibwas, who was noted for having stopped an uprising some years earlier. He is flanked by High Up in the Sky, Crossing the Wind, Little Wolf, and In-ne-ne-si.

AN ADOBE
PUEBLO IN
SAINT LOUIS

This replica of a traditional adobe pueblo is incongruously supplied with electrical wires and lights. Peopled by Zunis and Hopis, the exhibit provided spectators with closeup looks at the daily life and colorful ceremonies of Indians of the Southwest.

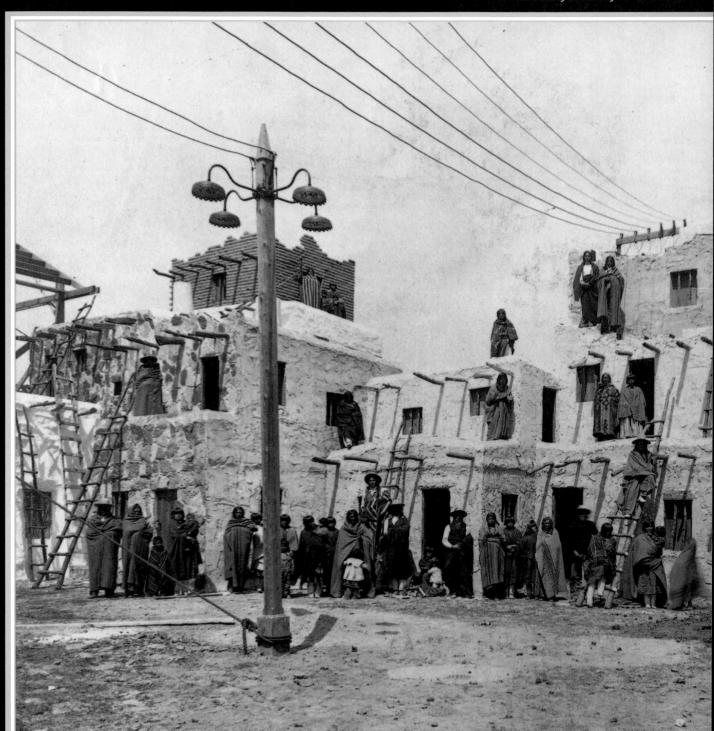

Pictured with friends from her tribe (above), Genevieve Cajiti, a Pueblo Indian, balances a water jar on her head, aided by a ring running through her hair. The ancestral costumes for both young women shown here include deerskin leggings, originally adopted as a defense against rattlesnake bites.

With artificial reptiles clenched between their teeth, Zuni and Hopi men (below) perform the Snake Dance, a prayer for rain. Fairgoers were said to prefer the more colorful kachina ceremony, in which dancers wore buffalo heads and deer heads.

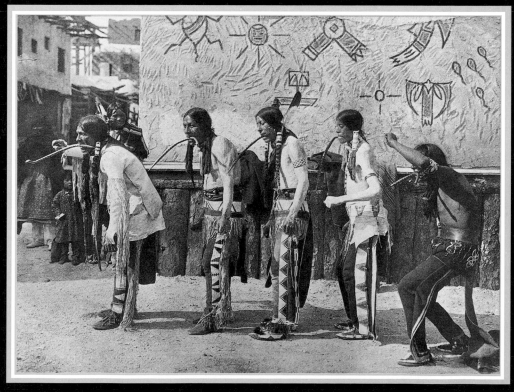

INTIMATIONS
OF LIFE ON
THE PLAINS

The Arapahos below, standing next to a tipi encircled by a brush windbreak, belong to a tribe that in the 18th century fought Comanches, Kiowas, and whites for dominance of the lower Plains. The group includes Mr. White Shirt (center), named for his dogged adherence to white men's clothes, and Cut Nose (far right), who was made reservation chief because he was a friend to whites.

An Oglala Sioux named Leading Hawk (far left) and his family are resplendent in ceremonial finery worn for a photograph. One observer complained that the Sioux, once lords of the northern Plains, "do not weave blankets or make pottery," but acknowledged that nobody matched "the vigor of their war dances."

Plumed for a war dance and armed with lance and shield, an Oglala Sioux named Comes Out Holy (below) poses astride a pinto pony. Obliging numerous photographers must have been onerous for many of the Indians, but especially so for a proud Oglala, heir to the tradition of great chiefs such as Crazy Horse and Red Cloud.

IMAGES OF
THE NORTHWEST
COAST

Towering totem poles, emblematic of the Northwest Coast tribes, flank the Alaska state building in an area of the fair removed from the Native American section. Carved with images of animals considered sacred and protective of a clan, the poles stood outside the homes of many Northwest Coast groups, as they do the Haida dwelling here.

Klalish, or Whale on the Beach (left), a
Kwakiutl from Vancouver Island, prepares
to demonstrate a skin-piercing ritual of his
tribe's ancient war dance. In the actual ritual, he would have been suspended from
ropes hooked to his skin. Here, however,
ropes were attached to a camouflaged
wooden frame to provide the "suspension."

The large carved mask below, with its long
hair of twisted cedar bark, is the Kwakiutl
version of the Raven. The mask was used in
that tribe's Hamatsa Dance, the most important rite of the Kwakiutl winter ceremonies.
The Raven, teacher and trickster, is a key figure in the cultures of many Northwest tribes.

Mrs. Emma George, a Nootka from Vancouver Island, British Columbia, weaves a basket
from cedar bark and grass, using the same
techniques and patterns passed down by her
ancestors. By this time, Northwest Coast Indians were already producing such wares to
sell to tourists, and it seems likely that Mrs.
George sold hers to world's fair visitors.

DEMONSTRATING A DESERT EXISTENCE

Mrs. Vincent Begay (above), a Navajo, holds her sleeping baby, who is bound to a cradleboard. Navajos built their own traditional mud-and-straw hogans to live in at the fair, and the women wove the blankets for which they were famous.

Mrs. Henry Boatman (left), a Maricopa, came to the fair with some 20 others from the Arizona desert—Maricopas, Pimas, and Papagos (Tohono O'odham). All three tribes won renown at the exposition for their ability to create excellent pots and baskets.

Cocopas from Baja California pose with the fair's W. J. McGee (center). The Cocopas brought all the tools and materials for building their homes as well as their own, pre-Columbian strains of corn and beans.

TAKING THE INDIAN DETOUR

Symbol of the tourist invasion, a locomotive fashioned by a Santa Clara Pueblo potter chugs along an imaginary track, followed by a tender and caboose (above). Opposite, Detourists pause beside their Harvey car to bargain with some local craftsmen.

"Come to the land of history and mystery!" urged the travel brochure for the Atchison, Topeka and Santa Fe Railroad. The year was 1926, and the vaunted destination was the land of the Indians—the pueblo villages and reservations of New Mexico and Arizona. "Get off the beaten track, take a detour through spectacular Indian country," said the promotion, which promised exotic scenery, comfortable accommodations, and the sight of authentic Indians making crafts and performing ceremonies in their villages. To help sell the tours—and thereby increase its business on the Chicago-Los Angeles route—the railroad provided hundreds of travel agents with a travelogue of glass lantern slides, examples of which are shown here and on the following pages.

These tours began at trackside. Known collectively as the Indian Detour, they took railroad passengers by car to visit the Navajo, Zuni, and Hopi reservations, as well as the pueblos of the Rio Grande Valley, and returned them several days later to the railroad. The Indian Detour opened the remote southwestern Indian lands to tourism for the first time. The cars, provided by the Fred Harvey Company, were a cross between a limousine and a school bus, a kind of stretched Model T, as one historian described them. "The biggest thing I ever saw!" recalls one elderly Navajo man, who remembers as a boy the long brown cars with the Harvey Company insignia on the side, nosing around the reservation. The so-called Detourists spent their days visiting reservations, ranches, and ancient ruins and their nights dining and dancing in luxury hotels built by the Fred Harvey Company.

The southwestern Indians soon discovered that the Detourists were eager to buy their crafts and began making items specifically for the tourist trade. A number of these objects, such as gourd rattles, kachina dolls, and fetishes, were originally designed for religious ceremonies, but the Indians fashioned nonreligious versions of them for sale, examples of which accompany the lantern slides on these pages. Native American creativity responded to tourist demands, and the southwestern Indian arts and crafts industry was born.

NAVIGATING NAVAJO LAND

Travel agents enticed tourists with landscapes of rugged beauty, such as Arizona's Canyon de Chelly (below), on the Navajo Reservation. For a more "native" experience, Detourists could choose optional horseback tours with camping under the stars.

A Navajo family in front of its hogan (right) smiles obligingly for the camera. The Santa Fe Railroad dispatched dozens of photographers to capture the beauty and friendliness of the Indian Southwest, and even provided darkrooms for them aboard the trains.

Navajo blankets were already famous by the 1920s, but until the Indian Detour, few tourists had ever seen them being woven on a typical outdoor loom (below). Navajo weavers switched from making blankets for their own use to producing them for sale.

Taboos against representing Navajo gods, or "ye'iis," in a permanent way discouraged many weavers from making rugs such as the one below. Ye'iis had previously been pictured only in ceremonial sand paintings, which were immediately destroyed after use.

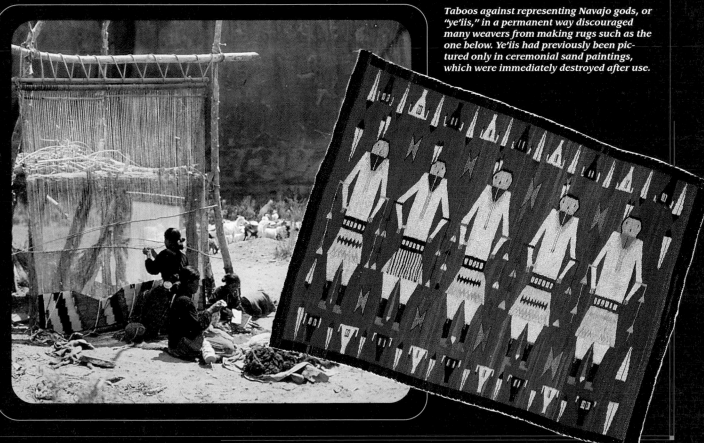

SAMPLING
THE CHARMS
OF THE PUEBLOS

Thunder Mountain, a sacred site of the Zuni, looms on the horizon beyond Zuni Pueblo (above), in western New Mexico. Spectacular scenery and convenient transportation drew railroad travelers to this previously isolated reservation.

A potter of Laguna Pueblo offers handcrafted items for sale (left). Although Pueblo Indians had no use for cups with handles and saucers in their own homes, they made them that way for the tourist trade, creating a much-needed source of income.

Employing a flywheel pump drill, a Zuni craftsman (below) bores a hole in a turquoise bead. The beads, often interspersed with tiny fetish carvings, were strung onto sinew for necklaces. Turquoise jewelry was highly prized by tourists.

Zuni fetishes such as the bear shown above were made for tourists in the late 1920s, although similar fetishes were still being used for religious purposes.

LIVING ARCHAEOLOGY AT A HOPI VILLAGE

Mishongnovi (below), a Hopi village in northern Arizona, stands untouched by time in this glass lantern slide. Travel brochures encouraged tourists to "catch archaeology alive!" in the southwestern Indian Detour.

Hopi women coiled baskets and the flat ceremonial platters known as plaques (above) as they had always done, but now they made them as tourist souvenirs.

Tourist kachina dolls such as the one at left resembled the dolls Hopis made for their children to introduce them to the symbolism of the supernatural beings, the kachinas.

RUINS AND RITUALS ON THE RIO GRANDE

A potter from the Rio Grande pueblo of Tesuque (below) kneads clay to make more of the "rain gods" lined up on her right. These figurines were sold as trinkets for tourists and never had any religious significance.

The Eagle Dance (above) at San Ildefonso Pueblo in New Mexico attracted hundreds of tourists eager to witness authentic Indian ceremonies at a time when many religious rituals were outlawed by the U.S. government.

Tesuque "rain god" figures such as this one (left) were mass-produced for tourists during the 1920s. Thousands of them were packed into boxes of candy as a marketing ploy.

The ancient ruins at Frijoles Canyon (above) in Bandelier National Monument were a popular tourist attraction in 1926. The Tewa-speaking peoples of the Rio Grande pueblos claim this region as their ancestral homeland.

2

WALKING THE WHITE MAN'S ROAD

An Osage delegation gathers in Washington, D.C., in the early 1890s shortly before oil was discovered on their Oklahoma reservation. By insisting that all minerals remain communal property, the Osage ensured that oil royalties would be shared by the entire tribe. After allotment, Osage "surplus" land was offered for sale through advertisements like this one (top left).

Early that morning, the Indians began their preparations. The men who were to do the killing smeared their faces with paint, decorated the manes and tails of their ponies with colored cloth, and took up their guns or bows and arrows. The women hitched the horses to the travois that would carry the smallest children and bring home the meat. All the preparations were made for a buffalo hunt, but bison would not be the quarry. It was beef-issue day on the Cheyenne-Arapaho Reservation, an event that took place every other Monday during the 1880s at 10 different stations on the land set aside for the two tribes between the Canadian and Red Rivers in the western Indian Territory.

By hunting the cattle as if they were buffalo, these Southern Arapahos and Southern Cheyennes were clinging to a vestige of their former culture while doing their best to make the transition to the white man's way of life. They now lived under the watchful eye of an Indian agent working for the U.S. Bureau of Indian Affairs. Each of the 10 issue stations on the Cheyenne-Arapaho Reservation had a blacksmith to shoe their horses and repair the farm tools they were learning to use, a farming instructor to teach them agriculture and animal husbandry, and a corral to hold the beef cattle. The Arapaho had no word for cattle in their language. They called the animal *wohaw*—because they had heard the white settlers yelling "whoa!" and "haw!" as they drove their teams of oxen across the prairie.

Reservation people turned events such as the beef-issue days into something uniquely Indian. An Arapaho who grew up on the reservation and took the name Carl Sweezy when he began school recalled how his people made a celebration of a mundane occurrence. "Issue days were big times for all of us," Sweezy said. "All across the prairies, people in bright colors and high spirits came riding to the issue station. There were visiting and excitement and work and feasting ahead for everyone. One by one as the clerk stamped the ration tickets of the heads of families, the men in the corral drove a beef from the pen and sent it down the chute. Yelling and racing his pony and with his family coming along behind as close as they could

Each reservation family kept a ration card, which the women commonly stored in beaded leather purses (above). The card was marked by the agent each time goods were issued. In the photograph at top left, Sioux gather at a corral on the Standing Rock Reservation in South Dakota to collect their weekly supply of beef. After the cattle were slaughtered, the women cleaned the animals' entrails, just as they used to do with buffalo (bottom left).

manage to do, the man rode after his wohaw as it bellowed and plunged and tore across the prairie, trying to escape. Wohaw could run almost as fast and bellow and turn almost as wildly as the buffalo once did. For a few hours, the Arapaho knew once more some of the excitement of the old buffalo hunt. And when at last the beef was shot down, the women moved in with their knives and kettles, skinning the hide off and cutting up the meat to take back to their lodges. Everybody had a piece of the raw liver, fresh and warm, before the families set out for home. Then, fires were kindled, and the feasting began." Similar wohaw "hunts" took place on the reservations of other Plains tribes. Like many other practices that linked the Indians to the past, these events were eventually banned. "A fearful hindrance to the work of civilization," the U.S. commissioner of Indian affairs, Thomas Jefferson Morgan, concluded in 1890, "it cannot but serve to perpetuate in a savage breast all the cruel and wicked propensities of his nature." Morgan ordered his agents to erect slaughterhouses for butchering the cattle.

The Indians objected strenuously. Many Cheyenne and Arapaho families went hungry until their leaders finally bowed to authority. "The sport that had been as important as the feasting on issue days was ended with that change from beef on the hoof to beef on the block," Sweezy wryly recalled. "Progress was catching up with us."

Just as Carl Sweezy's people put their own stamp on the harvesting of government issue beef, Indians everywhere attempted to preserve elements of cherished traditions within a reservation system designed to stamp out all vestiges of their old ways. Although reservations varied in size—from tracts of less than 100 acres in California to the immense 17-million-acre Navajo Reservation that sprawled over parts of Arizona, New Mexico, Colorado, and Utah—they had much in common. Each tribe was subjected in varying degrees to the repressive effects of an imposed, alien way of life. "We had to learn to live by farming instead of by hunting and trading," Sweezy said, "from people who did not speak our language or try to learn it, except for a few words, though they expected us to learn theirs."

The Indians saw their sacred ceremonies suppressed, their political structures undermined, their economic patterns transformed, and their children wrenched away from homes to be educated in boarding schools far from the influences of family and community. In addition to this array of efforts to "civilize" them, in many regions the Indians came under intense pressure from government officials and private entrepreneurs to sell their land for cattle grazing, mining speculation, mechanized agriculture, railroad building, timber cutting, or other white business interests.

Although many reservations comprised land that was part of a tribe's original domain, in many cases more than one group of Indians occupied the same space. By the 1880s, the Indian Territory had become a patchwork of 21 different reservations accommodating at least 67 different tribes. The Southern Arapaho were fortunate to share a reservation with old friends, the Southern Cheyenne. The way in which fate consigned the two tribes to the nearly 5,500-square-mile tract was a typical Indian story. They were confined to the area after they reluctantly accepted the terms of the Treaty of Medicine Lodge in 1867. In size, the reservation represented less than five percent of the territory both tribes had accepted at the great peace conference at Fort Laramie, Wyoming, in 1851. There the government had agreed that the Arapaho and Cheyenne should forever control all of the land from the North Platte River south to the Arkansas River and east of the Rocky Mountains through Colorado into western Kansas and including parts of Nebraska and Wyoming—more than 122,000 square miles. But the Pike's Peak gold rush of 1858 put the lie to that arrangement, as tens of thousands of white fortune seekers swarmed into Indian lands. The Southern Arapaho and Southern Cheyenne ended their resistance to the massive white intrusion after the infamous Sand Creek Massacre in 1864 in which scores of their women and children were slaughtered by Colonel John M. Chivington's 3rd Colorado Cavalry Regiment.

On their reservation in what is today Oklahoma, according to Sweezy, "Wind and rain and rivers and heat and cold and even some of the plants and animals were different from what we had always known." Even so, the Southern Arapaho were more fortunate in one sense than their cousins, the Northern Arapaho. When the Northern Arapaho were finally subdued in 1878, the U.S. government sent them to the Wind River Reservation in Wyoming, home of the group's bitterest enemies, the Eastern Shoshone, who had helped the Americans quell the Northern Arapaho during the last of the Plains wars.

Washakie, the principal Eastern Shoshone chief, had already discovered that his people's long history of friendship with whites counted for little when it came to land. He spoke for many reservation Indians when he said: "The white man, who possesses this whole vast country from sea to sea, who roams over it at pleasure, and lives where he likes, cannot know the cramp we feel in this little spot, with the undying remembrance. . .that every foot of what you proudly call America, not very long ago belonged to

This drawing is a symbolic representation of the band of 84 families led by the Oglala Sioux chief Big Road who came to live on the Standing Rock Reservation in the early 1880s. Each family or sub-band is identified by a name glyph attached to its head. The numbers were added later.

the red man. The Great Spirit gave it to us. There was room enough for all his many tribes, and all were happy in their freedom. But the white man had, in many ways we know not of, learned some things we had not learned; among them, how to make superior tools and terrible weapons, better for war than bows and arrows; and there seemed no end to the hordes of men that followed them from other lands beyond the sea. And so, at last, our fathers were steadily driven out, or killed, and we, their sons, but sorry remnants of tribes once mighty, are cornered in little spots of the

The church and buildings of the Warm Springs Indian Agency sprout from a hillside in northern Oregon in this early-20th-century photograph. The various Indian groups placed there under an 1855 treaty made with the Wasco are known collectively as the Confederated Tribes of Warm Springs.

earth all ours of right—cornered like guilty prisoners, and watched by men with guns, who are more than anxious to kill us off."

Prohibited from following the old Indian road yet unable to follow the new path of the white man, many Indians lost their way and fell into idleness and drink. "I do not wish to be shut up in a corral," complained Sitting Bull, the Sioux leader who triumphed at the Battle of the Little Bighorn. "It is bad for young men to be fed by an agent. It makes them lazy and drunken. All agency Indians I have seen are worthless. They are neither red warriors nor white farmers."

Yet most Indians adapted to the new life, accommodating themselves when it was prudent, resisting when they could. They created new institutions to help them survive and ultimately transformed their reservations into cultural enclaves that permitted them to preserve their identity.

In 1881 the Bureau of Indian Affairs administered no fewer than 102 reservations west of the Mississippi containing about 224,000 Indians. The key supervisor on each reservation was the Indian agent. In the West, the first group of agents were mainly former army officers. But in January 1870, Congress banned the employment of military retirees in this capacity because of its concern that their presence might incite the Indians. President Ulysses S. Grant, as part of his peace policy regarding the western tribes, turned to churchmen chosen from the major religious denominations doing missionary work among the tribes. Grant hoped that such men would relate well to the Indians and put an end to widespread agency corruption. When Grant's presidency ended in 1877, however, the church-sponsored agents were largely replaced by political appointees. By the 1890s, almost half of the agents were, once again, retired army officers.

Working from his agency—the reservation's official hub, which typically consisted of an office building, houses for staff, storehouses, and a school—the agent managed the clerks, blacksmiths, teachers, and farming instructors whose task it was to Americanize the Indians. The agent also was responsible for enforcing the law, controlling the use of the land, and administering tribal funds.

One fondly remembered Quaker appointee was Brinton Darlington, the original agent at the Cheyenne-Arapaho Reservation. "He had not been trained in our religious societies and did not know our ceremonies," wrote Carl Sweezy. "But he did not try to wipe them all out, as some white people believed in doing. He was patient and kind; he managed like a chief; he prayed to the Man Above when he was thankful and when he

needed power." When Darlington died in 1872, Sweezy said, "Cheyenne and Arapaho chiefs, as well as white men, wept over his grave." Few of the agents, however, were as well intentioned and competent as Darlington.

One of the agent's main tasks was the allocation of the annuities guaranteed to the Indians by treaty. These payments, which compensated the Indians for relinquishing their lands and were intended to tide them over until they achieved self-sufficiency, took the form of both cash and goods. For a large tribe such as the Lakota, or Western Sioux, annual payments could run as high as $100,000. The money was disbursed on a per capita basis, usually in the form of gold or silver coins. Everyone gathered at the agency from many miles around, bringing their tipis with them and making a holiday of the occasion. While children played hoop and stick and other games, adults visited, feasted, and gambled. Dozens of white traders who traveled from reservation to reservation also showed up to hawk their wares.

Distribution of food and goods occurred frequently, sometimes every week. Most agents issued coupons as certificates of eligibility, and the women sewed little beaded pockets from animal skins to protect them. "When the goods were distributed," recalled Carl Sweezy, "everyone put on something new—a blanket or a hat or a coat or a shirt or a shawl. If a man got a pair of shoes or trousers that he did not want, he sold them or

Blackfeet families receive old clothing, blankets, and boots on their reservation in northern Montana. The government began issuing supplies to the Blackfeet in 1883 after the buffalo disappeared from the northern Plains.

This cotton dress from the Fort Berthold Reservation in North Dakota is typical of the clothing worn by late-19th-century Indian women. Agents distributed fabric, needles, and thread so that women could make clothes for themselves and their families.

traded them off for something he fancied for himself or his family. There was trading going on everywhere."

Some whites thought of rations as a kind of dole, confirming the relationship formulated by Chief Justice John Marshall back in 1831 when he described the tribes as "domestic dependent nations [whose] relation to the United States resembles that of a ward to his guardian." The Indians, on the other hand, did not consider themselves wards of the government. They regarded rations as their just due and agreed with the Oglala Sioux chief Red Cloud when he declared, "The white man owes us a living for the lands he has taken from us."

The distribution of goods afforded lucrative possibilities for dishonest agents. In collusion with corrupt contractors who paid kickbacks, they handed out shoes with paper soles, sacks of short-weighted grain, blankets that ripped easily, and shovels that bent like tin. Some agents held back supplies and sold them to traders. One favorite scam was run in cooperation with crooked cattle dealers. The agent paid the dealer top dollar for scrawny stock and took a split of the profits. The dealer then arranged to repurchase the cattle at lower prices or even to rustle them. He then drove the herd on to another reservation to reap further profits with another corrupt agent. Other avenues awaited the unscrupulous. Some agents skimmed off annuity payments or sold the rights to graze cattle on the reservation, harvest timber, or extract minerals. The agent on the Apache reservation at San Carlos in the Arizona Territory spent his time in a private mining venture; another agent in the Southwest stocked his own ranch with government cattle. With such shenanigans in mind, Civil War hero and Indian fighter General William T. Sherman defined a reservation as a "parcel of land set aside for Indians, surrounded by thieves."

Progress in the centerpiece of Americanization—that is, making Indians self-supporting through agriculture—varied by region. Many tribes, of course, had been cultivating the soil for centuries. The Cherokee, Choctaw, Chickasaw, Creek, and Seminole—the so-called Five Civilized Tribes—farmed in the Indian Territory as they had in their ancestral homelands in the Southeast. The Navajo on their large reservation in the Southwest recovered from their grueling four-year exile at Bosque Redondo and made the desert bloom. In 1879, a decade after their

Members of a traveling medicine show, probably white men dressed as Plains Indians, wait for customers outside their booth, a small tipi, in 1941. The "paw maw" on the placard is a misspelling of powwow, an Algonquian word for medicine man. Whites have ascribed special powers and natural medical knowledge to Indians since early times.

return, gardens, grainfields, orchards, and sheep herds provided almost all their subsistence. Agent John C. Pyle, reporting that only six percent of Navajo supplies came from the government, bragged, "A Navajo with a sharp stick and hoe can get from one-third to one-half more returns than white men with the best machinery."

On the Great Plains, however, farming was a different story. Federal officials had optimistically expected the Plains Indians to make the transition to self-supporting agriculture before the buffalo disappeared. But growing crops and raising livestock were alien activities to a nomadic hunting people accustomed to living in bands with their tipis side by side. "Even our tribal leaders, great men at hunting and fighting and conducting social gatherings and religious ceremonies, knew nothing about how to prepare ground or what seed to plant. . .or how to plant and cultivate and harvest and store crops," wrote Carl Sweezy. "To us it seemed unsociable and lonely, and not the way people were meant to live."

The environment was also a problem. The growing season on the northern Plains was short, and on the southern Plains, searing heat and lack of water withered the crops. The plants that reached full growth were often consumed by grasshoppers and other pests. John D. Miles, the agent who replaced Brinton Darlington on the Cheyenne-Arapaho Reservation,

These labels from 19th-century patent medicines capitalize on two popular Indian stereotypes—the noble warrior and the tender-hearted maiden. The manufacturer of Red Jacket Stomach Bitters alleged that the recipe came from the late-18th-century Seneca chief himself.

concluded that a white farmer would "starve to death if placed on 160 acres or even a section of the lands in this country." A Kiowa chief named Little Mountain advised his agent that if the president of the United States wanted the Indians to raise corn, he should send them some land suitable for growing it.

Unable to feed themselves and denied sufficient rations by a penny-pinching Congress, many Plains Indians suffered terribly. For many years after the buffalo disappeared (the great herds were gone from the southern Plains in 1878 and vanished from the northern Plains in 1884), conditions of starvation existed on many Plains reservations.

A few Indians managed to get off the reservations by performing in the Wild West shows staged by William F. "Buffalo Bill" Cody and other entrepreneurs during the 1880s. But government officials frowned on such employment as a glorification of the Indians' warrior past.

About this time, federal authorities made another move aimed at controlling the Indians. Worried about the threat of rebellion by hungry Plains tribes, Congress approved a request from the Interior Department to organize an Indian police force. Appointing Indians to oversee their fellow

A souvenir program depicts a settler and an Indian on opposite sides of Cody. When Sitting Bull first saw the sharpshooter Annie Oakley perform, featured here as a "champion markswoman," he named her Watanya Cicilia—Little Sure Shot.

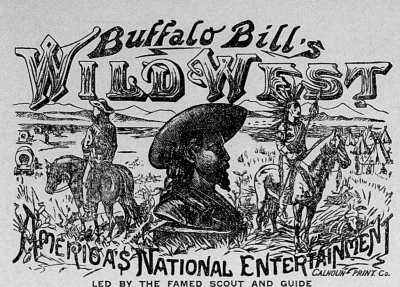

This telegram grants the Lakota chief Sitting Bull permission to leave the reservation. Before taking Indians abroad, Cody had to post bonds with the U.S. government guaranteeing their safe return.

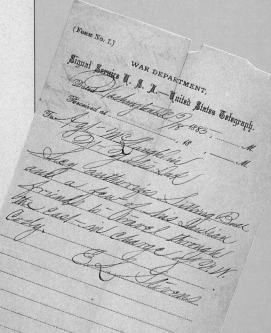

PLAYACTING FOR BUFFALO BILL

Between 1883 and 1911, hundreds of Plains Indians helped William F. Cody win international fame and create the romanticized image of the American West by performing in his immensely successful touring show, Buffalo Bill's Wild West. Recruited from various reservations at a time when many tribes were struggling to survive, the Indians, mainly Sioux, Cheyenne, Arapaho, Kiowa, and Pawnee, reenacted outlawed ceremonies and staged pony races, buffalo hunts, and mock attacks that thrilled audiences throughout the United States, Canada, and Europe.

Cody preferred Indians who had had minimal contact with whites. Although the Indians themselves welcomed the opportunity to earn money and see the world, many Indian rights advocates accused Cody of exploitation. The shows, said one critic, "teach the Indian that what the white man really wants of him is amusement furnished by exhibitions of picturesque barbarism."

For his four-month stint with the Wild West in 1885, the legendary Sitting Bull received $50 per week, a bonus of $125, and the exclusive right to sell his portraits and autograph. This photograph was taken while the troupe was performing in Montreal, Canada.

MOCK ATTACKS AND STAGED RITUALS

Wearing war bonnets and brandishing lances, Indian warriors dance menacingly in a simulated camp in Omaha, Nebraska, probably in 1908. In the foreground are two white female captives. The scene was part of the reenactment of the so-called Battle of Summit Springs, an 1869 incident in which Cody helped rescue some captured settlers and allegedly shot and killed a Cheyenne war chief named Tall Bull.

Against a backdrop of painted mountains, a group of Sioux perform a "dog-eating" ceremony in Madison Square Garden in the early 1900s. Such spectacles served to confirm white stereotypes of Indians as a "dying race" of exotic savages, the perfect foil for mythical white heroes like Buffalo Bill.

ON TOUR AT HOME AND ABROAD

While Buffalo Bill's Wild West extravaganza brought the western frontier to the world, it also introduced hundreds of reservation Indians to foreign sights they could only imagine, such as this view of the Pacific Ocean and the Cliff House from a beach in San Francisco (below). During a tour of Venice in the 1890s, Cody and four Indians went sightseeing in a gondola (top left). In England, others (bottom left) posed in their full show regalia at Land's End, Cornwall. The show was so hugely popular that it inspired European royalty such as Prince Albert of Monaco, pictured at right with Cody and some Indian friends in Cody, Wyoming, to visit America and see the Indians firsthand in their western homeland.

tribesmen solved the problem of having to muster U.S. Army troops every time there was a disturbance. In addition to handling domestic disputes and cases of cattle rustling and horse theft, the police acted as the agent's handymen. They kept the agent abreast of current gossip, carried messages, took the census, chased after children truant from school, and performed dozens of other chores. Control of drunkenness—and of bootleggers, moonshiners, and the peddlers of alcoholic patent medicine—was a chronic problem. According to one estimate, up to 95 percent of the crimes committed on the reservations were attributable to alcohol.

Policing appealed to many Indians. It not only gave them a job but also enabled them to play a role similar to one performed in the old days when Dog Soldiers (camp police) from the warrior societies kept order during the communal buffalo hunts, migrations, and great summer gatherings. The pay authorized by Congress was meager—in the beginning, $8 per month for officers and $5 for privates. The blue uniforms seldom fit properly, faulty pistols frequently misfired, and recruits had to provide their own horses. Indian police, moreover, often had to endure insults from fellow tribesmen who saw them as traitors. On one occasion, Lakota warriors at the Lower Brulé Reservation threatened to kill anyone who volunteered for the police. But young men eager to carry arms joined up. By 1890 a total of nearly 800 Indian policemen were in service on practically every reservation in the United States. They had to keep their hair cut short and were expected to set an example by wearing non-Indian garb off-duty and their uniforms during duty hours. The brass buttons on the uniforms featured the stamped figure of an Indian guiding a plow and the legend "God helps those who help themselves."

The police role grew larger in 1883. The secretary of the interior, Henry M. Teller, was distressed at the persistence of "certain of the old heathenish dances" on the reservations. These practices, he wrote, "are intended and calculated to stimulate the warlike passions." He also deplored plural mar-

A Blackfeet police-man, photographed in 1902, wears the black hat, blue cloth uniform, and brass buttons of his office. Each button, one of which is shown at left with a typical Indian police badge, contained an image of a man plowing a field and the words "God helps those who help themselves." Indian policemen also carried night sticks, like the one shown above, and usually pistols.

riages and the continued influence of medicine men. Henceforth, Indian police were ordered to prevent the performance of traditional ceremonies. The new orders put the police in a difficult position—one that would become even more sticky when they were called upon to enforce further directives from Washington banning long hair on all males, and even prohibiting social visiting because it was thought to produce idleness and vagrancy.

The 1883 directive banning the Sun Dance and other religious practices also provided for the creation of Indian courts in which these and other offenses could be tried. Until then, usually the agent adjudicated cases brought by the Indian police, although there were exceptions. On the Yakima Reservation in Washington State, for example, residents elected their own judges, using ballots of different colors to overcome the problem of illiteracy. Appeals of the judge's decision went up to the agent. The new Courts of Indian Offenses consisted at first of the three top-ranking police officials and later of three judges appointed by the agent.

Like elders on the old tribal councils, the Indian judges tended to compromise and conciliate. Courts rarely imprisoned an offender, partly because there were few suitable jails—a Paiute court ordered culprits chained to a tree in the absence of a cell. Instead, courts frequently prescribed forced labor. One year at the Tulalip Reservation in Washington State, Snohomish prisoners provided 1,366 days of badly needed roadwork. If the court called for a fine, it was usually levied in cash. On the Sioux reservations, however, judges seeking to disarm Indians who might create problems for the community demanded payment in guns; the Standing Rock Agency court collected 74 rifles and five revolvers in one year. As in the old days, judgments sometimes focused on compensation for the victim or kin. Thanks to the police and the court officials, most reservations were enclaves of order in a West notorious for lawlessness. In 1889 the agent for the Cheyenne-Arapaho Reservation in the Indian Territory reported, "No record exists in the office of any crimes having been committed by the Indians during the past year."

Major crimes lay beyond the scope of the Indian courts. Until 1883, such offenses had been handled by either military or federal tribunals. Then the U.S. Supreme Court considered the case of Crow Dog, who had been sentenced to death by a federal court for killing Spotted Tail, a chief of the Brulé Sioux at the Rosebud Reservation. The High Court ruled that the United States lacked jurisdiction over crimes committed between Indians on the reservation. The ruling strengthened the concept of tribal sovereignty, but only briefly. Two years later, Congress, outraged at the freeing of Crow Dog, passed legislation bringing murder, rape, arson, burglary, and other major crimes committed on the reservation under the purview of the relevant territory or state. The law was upheld by the Supreme Court the following year.

The case itself illustrated the undermining of the old tribal custom. Crow Dog belonged to a group opposed to Spotted Tail, a traditional chief whose authority once would have gone unquestioned. Crow Dog had been a captain of the Indian police force, an institution that helped erode traditional leadership. Agents promoted divisions as part of their program to Americanize the Indians. At the Pine Ridge Reservation, this involved the creation of many new white-approved chiefs to undercut the old— from 12 in 1878 to 63 only two years later. Most reservations split into two general groups: those who opposed change and those who accepted it.

Arranged by sex and age, Indian youngsters sit for a portrait at the Carlisle Indian Industrial School in 1884. The school opened in 1879 with 130 students, mainly Sioux. By 1900 there were 1,218 students from at least 76 tribes in attendance at the school.

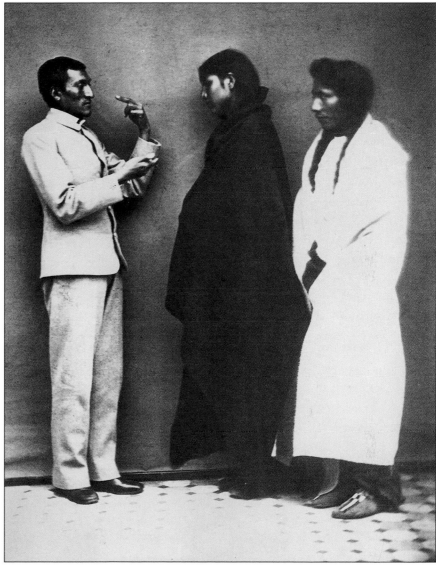

Con-way-how-nif, a Cheyenne student at Hampton Normal and Agricultural Institute in Virginia, welcomes two new students with sign language—the universal language of the Plains. Until students from different tribes mastered English, signing was their only means of communicating with one another.

Quanah Parker, the mixed-blood Comanche chief, was one of those rare leaders with a foot in each camp, who could urge his people to follow after the white way with regard to education and employment while adhering to the old Indian ways of dress and marriage.

No component of the Americanization program proved more controversial or divisive than education. Government officials and reformers regarded the schooling of young Indians as the linchpin of all their efforts. Alice Fletcher, an anthropologist active in various Indian rights organizations, expressed the credo of these well-meaning groups when she declared, "The task of converting the American Indian into the Indian American belongs to the Indian student."

The federal government's drive for formal schooling began in earnest during the 1870s. Until then, the only extensive Indian educational systems

Havasupai young-sters line up in front of their reservation school in 1900. Located in Arizona along the Colorado River, the reservation occupies a fertile branch of the Grand Canyon that has been cultivated by the tribe for at least 900 years.

Students of the Port Gamble Indian School in Puget Sound, Washington, pose on the porch of the schoolhouse. At the end of the 19th century, there were only enough schools in the Puget Sound area to serve one-third of the Indian children.

existed in the Indian Territory, where schools of the Five Civilized Tribes were financed by a combination of tribal, church, and federal funds. Before the Civil War, Cherokees had operated a highly successful system that was larger than the white systems in Arkansas and Missouri. Most of the schools on other reservations were maintained by missionaries. Then, in 1870, Congress authorized $100,000, the first large appropriation for general Indian education. The emphasis was on vocational training—farming and trades such as carpentry for boys and housekeeping for girls. At first education took place mostly at day schools, which allowed students to go home in the evening, although boarding schools also were started on some reservations to accommodate a widely scattered population.

But a growing number of theorists argued that education ought to take place in boarding schools far from the influences of home and reservation. The leading proponent of the off-reservation boarding school was former cavalry officer Richard Henry Pratt. In 1878 Pratt persuaded Samuel Chapman Armstrong, founder of Hampton Normal and Agricultural Institute in Virginia for black freedmen, to accept 17 newly released Indian prisoners of war from Fort Marion in Saint Augustine, Florida. The Indians had learned English and basic arithmetic while under Pratt's supervision.

The Hampton program became the model for a system of boarding schools organized to assimilate Indians into white society. The plan was fashioned after the curriculum developed for young African Americans—although the blacks and the Indians were, for the most part, kept segregated from one another. The program's hallmark was its "outing" feature, in which each Indian student lived for an extended period of time with a northern white family as a kind of total immersion course in "civilized" culture.

Pratt disagreed with the Hampton emphasis on instilling pride in their Indian heritage among the students. He was convinced that if the Indians were to integrate successfully into mainstream America they would have to reject their past completely. In 1879, hoping to put his concept into practice, Pratt persuaded the government to establish the Carlisle Indian Industrial School in the old cavalry barracks at Carlisle, Pennsylvania.

A headstone in a cemetery in Hampton, Virginia, marks the final resting place of a Sioux baby born to a Hampton Institute student and named after the school's founder, Samuel C. Armstrong. Disease claimed the lives of many Indian students and their families.

The school opened with 130 students, more than half of them recruited by Pratt himself from among the Sioux. One of the Lakotas from the Rosebud Reservation who traveled east that fall was 10-year-old Luther Standing Bear, who later confessed that he had volunteered "not knowing what it meant and not caring" but simply to prove his bravery to his father.

What awaited Luther Standing Bear and the other Indian children was a shock course in Americanization. Everyone at Carlisle had to speak English; on pain of corporal punishment, no tribal language was allowed without permission. The boys had their hair clipped to the skull. Both boys and girls were outfitted with uniforms, taught military drill, and subjected to weekly inspections. Each day was tightly regimented. Students spent half of the class time in reading, writing, and arithmetic and the other half in vocational pursuits. Boys learned agriculture, harness making, tinsmithing, printing, and other crafts; girls took up sewing, cooking, washing, ironing, and dressmaking. There was also regularly scheduled religious instruction.

Carlisle kept its students up to five years or more without allowing them to go home to visit their families. A Hampton-style outing was the culmination of Pratt's approach to integration—as he put it, the "supreme Americanizer." He also separated Indian children from kin and tribe at school. Pratt liked to preach to his audiences with reference to the practice of baptism by total immersion: "I am a Baptist, because I believe in immersing the Indians in our civilization and when we get them under, holding them there until they are thoroughly soaked."

Thanks to Pratt's skills as an organizer and promoter, Carlisle became the showplace of Indian education. Enrollment reached 1,218 and included students drawn from more than 76 different tribes. Pratt conducted tours, delivered speeches across the country, and sent his top students to Washington to be shown off to congressmen and other officials. Carlisle set the pattern for about two dozen additional boarding schools established off the reservation before the end of the century.

Students later wrote of their boarding school experiences with bitterness. "In those days, the Indian schools were like jails and run along military lines, with roll calls four times a day," recalled John Lame Deer, a Miniconjou Sioux. Another Sioux, Mildred Stinson, an Oglala, remembered that she was only seven years old when she arrived at boarding school. "There was nobody to say good night to me, and I remember I cried all night." Hundreds of students found the regimen so unbearable that they ran away. And yet former students would later write fondly of the way in which boarding schools, by bringing together youth from different tribes, fostered feelings of a common identity that would profoundly influence 20th-century Indian cultural renewal.

Boarding schools operating on the reservations copied the Carlisle model. One former student wrote: "Our belongings were taken from us, even the little medicine bags our mothers had given us to protect us from harm. Everything was placed in a heap and set afire." The obligatory hair shearing sometimes took place as part of a public ritual in which students had to renounce their Indian origins.

At many schools, Indian youngsters suffered an abnormally high mortality rate. Crowding together large numbers of young people with little resistance to infectious diseases created epidemics. Disease claimed the lives of 13 of the first 60 children sent to Carlisle from the Comanche and Kiowa reservation; half of the 24 Southern Ute students recruited for school in New Mexico died there or shortly after returning home.

Large numbers of Indian families refused to send their children to boarding school. To force them to comply with compulsory education requirements, agents sometimes jailed parents or withheld annuities or rations, a sanction formally authorized by Congress. Indian police conducted yearly roundups in which children were forcibly taken from their homes and sent off to school. On more than one occasion, they had to hold off mobs of angry family members at gunpoint. Some policemen resigned rather than participate. Although parents hated seeing their children leave—"When we put our children in school," said a Navajo mother, "it is like giving our hearts up"—many considered the ordeal worth all the heartache if it enabled their offspring to succeed on terms dictated by white society. But others saw education differently, regarding it as the armor necessary to defend tribal identity. Geronimo, the great Chiricahua Apache war leader, actually ordered his nephew to attend Carlisle. The nephew, Asa Daklugie, later explained the logic of his famous uncle's decision: "Without this training in the ways of the White Eyes, our people could never compete with them. So it was necessary that those destined for leadership prepare themselves to cope with the enemy."

Students who endured the boarding school regimen usually encountered new trials after graduation. Although a few found a place in the white world, the vast majority returned to the reservation, where they found themselves in limbo between cultures. They seldom found suitable work and too often learned that the knowledge and skills they had struggled to acquire had little relevance on the reservation. "We come out half red and half white, not knowing what we are," said John Lame Deer.

Prayer bundles hang from poles outside a Hidatsa cabin on the Fort Berthold Reservation in North Dakota in 1908. Despite prohibitions against traditional religion, many Indians, especially those living in remote areas, continued personal observances.

"There was no happy gathering of family and friends, as I had so fondly dreamed there might be," a Shawnee graduate of Hampton recalled. "Instead of being eager to learn the new ideas I had to teach them, they gave me to understand very plainly that they did not approve of me. I had no real home to go to, and my relatives did not welcome my presence."

Many came home alienated from the old ways. Don Talayesva, a Hopi returning from the Sherman Institute in Riverside, California, discovered that "education had spoiled me for making a living in the desert. I was not hardened to heavy work in the heat and dust, and I did not know how to get rain, control winds, or even predict good and bad weather." When Sun Elk, renamed Rafael, came home to Taos Pueblo in New Mexico after seven years at Carlisle, the chiefs complained to his father: "He has not learned the things that Indian boys should learn. He has no hair. He has no blankets. He cannot even speak our language, and he has a strange smell. He is not one of us." Sun Elk let his hair grow long and put on the breechcloth again, but only after he married a Taos Pueblo woman was he fully accepted.

A group of Ojibwas removed from the Mille Lacs region of Minnesota pose with their leader, Round Earth (back row, third from right), in 1905. They were among the many Ojibwa communities forced to live on the White Earth Reservation at a time when timber interests were gaining control of their lands.

Indian resistance and second thoughts by whites caused enthusiasm for off-reservation schools to wane during the 1890s. Congress in 1894 approved a measure prohibiting removal of Indian children beyond the limits of the reservation without parental consent. Advocates of educating children on the reservation began to be heard. They argued that an education close to home would eliminate the gulf that yawned between students sent far away and the people they left behind. Schools closer to home, they believed, would favorably influence the tribe as a whole. Only older students who had completed school on the reservation would be sent away for advanced studies. By the turn of the 20th century, fewer than one-third of Indian students were attending school off the reservation. Overall, despite an increase in enrollment of more than sixfold during the previous 25 years, about half of all Indian children still did not attend any kind of school.

In September 1878, a band of about 300 Northern Cheyennes who had been placed among the Southern Cheyenne on the Cheyenne-Arapaho Reservation in the Indian Territory broke out and headed northward in a desperate attempt to return to their native Wyoming and Montana. Led by the warrior Dull Knife, the Indians crossed lands that now included ranches, roads, and railroads. A few of the Cheyennes succeeded in reaching Montana, but most were either killed or arrested by a pursuing force of cavalry. The government ordered the survivors sent back to the Indian Territory, but they refused. While held at Fort Robinson, Nebraska, in January

Salish chief Charlot (center) sits with his counselors in Washington, D.C. The delegation had traveled to the capital to secure permanent rights to the Bitterroot Valley. Although the Salish won temporary concessions, the tribe was forced to move to the Flathead Reservation in western Montana in 1891.

1879, the group of about 150 men, women, and children made a dash for freedom. One-third of them were mercilessly shot and killed by the garrison force. The massacre provoked a public outcry all across America. One newspaper called it a "dastardly outrage upon humanity and a lasting disgrace to our boasted civilization." The struggle by Dull Knife's band resulted in the Northern Cheyenne's being assigned to a reservation in their Montana homeland five years later.

The same month as the slaughter of the Northern Cheyennes, a band of Ponca Indians attracted national attention. The Ponca were an agricultural people from the area around the Niobrara River along the Nebraska-South Dakota border who had never fought against the United States. Yet in 1876 they were ordered to relocate in the Indian Territory, where they suffered terribly. The soil was too poor for crops, and there was little forage for livestock. During the first three years on the reservation, about one-fourth of the tribe died of starvation and disease, including the son of a Ponca chief named Standing Bear. Determined to bury his son along the banks of the Niobrara, Standing Bear and a small band of followers fled the reservation. They made it through Kansas but were captured in Nebraska and imprisoned at Fort Omaha. On learning of his real purpose in returning to Nebraska, many whites sympathized with Standing Bear. Two Omaha attorneys agreed to defend him in court. In a landmark decision, U.S. District judge Elmer S. Dundy ruled in favor of Standing Bear, claiming that Indians had certain rights under the law and could not be prevented from returning to their original homelands. Dundy's ruling contributed heavily to the eventual erosion of the reservation system.

After his court victory, Standing Bear traveled east with a crusading newspaperman named Thomas Henry Tibbles to publicize the evils of the reservations. Joining them were two articulate Omaha Indians, sister and half brother Susette and Francis La Flesche. In Chicago, Boston, New York, Philadelphia, and Washington, D.C., huge and receptive audiences listened to their message of condemnation. For the first time, large numbers of whites became aware of the Indians' lamentable situation, and public opinion, especially in the East, began to turn against the reservation system.

In the meantime, a few tribes kept up their attempts to escape the confinement imposed by the whites. Bands of Chiricahua Apaches repeatedly fled the San Carlos Reservation in southwestern Arizona to wage guerrilla warfare from mountain redoubts across the border in Mexico. The Chiricahua resistance ended in 1886 with the surrender of the chief Geronimo. Not taking any chances, authorities sent Geronimo and more

A group of Kickapoos meet with their lawyers in 1889. With a long history of splintering and migration, the Kickapoo, originally from the Great Lakes region, finally settled down in the late 1880s; some groups ended up in Oklahoma, others in Kansas, and still others in Mexico.

than 340 others to exile in Florida. Geronimo was eventually transferred to Fort Sill, Oklahoma. He died there in 1909.

In the opinion of agent John Pickering, however, no tribe could match the obstinacy of the Southern Kickapoo in "tenaciously continuing to be Indians." Originally from the Great Lakes area, the Southern Kickapoo had migrated to Mexico in 1839 and lived there for more than three decades, periodically marauding across the border into Texas. In 1874, after U.S. cavalrymen smashed their settlements, nearly 400 Southern Kickapoos took up reluctant residence on a reservation in the central portion of the Indian Territory, where they began an unrelenting campaign of resistance to Americanization. Despite government grants of farm machinery and livestock, the men continued to hunt and trade, leaving the gardening to their wives and appropriating an occasional steer from the Texas herds that crossed the reservation. Against agency edicts, they continued with

their religious festivals, horse racing, and gambling. The Southern Kick-apoo bombarded agency officials with faultfinding. Every month or so the one literate member of the tribe, Johnson Warsano, fired off letters of complaint on behalf of the people: The ration flour was wormy; the agency blacksmith did shoddy work. As a U.S. Indian commissioner put it, the Southern Kickapoo were convinced that "had the Great Spirit intended them to become white men, he would so have created them." They refused to be counted in a census, thinking it part of a ruse to force their children into school. The government built a school, and after tribesmen threatened to burn it down, the building was converted to a storehouse. The Quakers finally managed to establish a school in 1890 with the support of a group of progressive Kickapoos who had migrated from their reservation in Kansas. Two-thirds of the tribe still refused to travel the white man's road. These recalcitrants were known to frustrated officials as Kicking Kickapoos.

On practically every reservation, people defied the prohibitions relating to traditional sacred beliefs. Medicine men practiced behind closed doors, and young men still stole off into the hills in quest of visions. Major rituals such as the Sun Dance took place in secrecy. Similarly, tribes on the

Instead of piercing their skin in the traditional manner, Lakota Sun Dancers on the Rosebud Reservation accommodate government regulations by attaching themselves to the center pole with a rope looped around their backs. Only men with scars from previous piercings had permission to participate in this imposed new version of the ritual.

western coast of Canada defied that government's ban on the potlatch ceremony, continuing this grand celebration featuring feasting and prodigious gift giving, which whites saw as wasteful and barbarous.

Many Indians developed new religious movements that combined Christianity with traditional native beliefs. The earliest of the reservation prophets was the Seneca Handsome Lake, who founded the Longhouse religion in 1799. He prescribed a code of conduct for his people on their reservation in New York State based on a series of dreams he experienced while deathly ill. The code encouraged education and farming, urged reverence for the sacred powers honored in the Seneca past, banned sexual promiscuity, and forbade excessive consumption of alcohol, which had afflicted his own life. His preachings still inspire the Seneca and kindred tribes.

Another new movement, founded at the opposite end of the continent on Washington's Puget Sound nearly a century later, fostered accommodation with white society. In 1881 Squsachtun, a baptized Catholic from the Coast Salish tribe called the Squaxin, started what became known as the Indian Shaker Church. Like Handsome Lake, Squsachtun, also known as John Slocum, returned from near death with a vision of salvation for his people. Squsachtun had a second brush with death, and he attributed his survival to a bedside phenomenon: an uncontrollable trembling that afflicted his attendant wife. Taking the Shaker name from this tremor, he preached a religion that blended such eclectic elements as the sign of the cross from Catholicism, simple wooden churches from Protestantism, sacred dancing from traditional Salish ceremonies, and the new ritual shaking to heal believers. The Shaker movement reached north into Canada and southward through reservations all the way into California.

Other prophets preached resistance to assimilation. Just as the reservation era was beginning in the Northwest during the 1860s, a short, hunchbacked medicine man by the name of Smohalla, who had begun his messianic career a decade earlier, emerged to oppose white domination. A member of the tiny Wanapum tribe in eastern Washington, Smohalla established the Dreamer cult, so called because of its practice of spending long periods of time in dreamlike states. He denounced the plowing of the earth as a sacrilege and predicted the rising up of Indians living and dead in a mighty force that would sweep away their white oppressors. His antiwhite influence became so pervasive that authorities attributed all Indian defiance in the region to Smohalla and his followers, even blaming them for the attempted flight to Canada in 1877 by Nez Percés who were intent upon avoiding confinement on a reservation.

Picket Pin, a Brulé Sioux, was one of a number of Indians on the Rosebud Reservation who did not approve of the Ghost Dance, brought to the Sioux from the Paiute prophet Wovoka in 1890. When Ghost Dancers left their log cabins to live in traditional tipi encampments, Picket Pin would dismantle their homes and sell the wood.

The most powerful new movement, the Ghost Dance, originated about 1870 among the Northern Paiute of Nevada. A holy man named Wodziwob—White Hair—prescribed a means by which his destitute tribesmen on the Walker River Reservation could bring back the old ways and resurrect the ghosts of their dead. For nights on end, he said, men, women, and children must join in circles and move in a shuffling step to the left while singing special songs. The movement failed to usher in the promised new age and ebbed in popularity. Then, in 1889, another Northern Paiute, Wovoka, also known as Jack Wilson, revived the movement. The son of one of Wodziwob's followers, Wovoka reported experiencing death and rebirth when the "sun died"—during a solar eclipse. This time, perhaps because the Indian's plight had grown worse in the previous two decades, the Ghost Dance flourished on reservations all across the West. Part of the appeal was Wovoka's prophecy that the white people would disappear if the Indians danced. Wovoka foresaw that this eradication of the enemy would occur as the result of some natural calamity. But by the time it reached the Pine Ridge Reservation in South Dakota in 1890, the Ghost Dance had assumed a more militant aspect. The Lakota Sioux were dispirited, hungry, and angry at the loss of additional lands to the government. "There was no hope on earth, and God seemed to have forgotten us," recalled Chief Red Cloud. "The people snatched at the hope."

Whites feared that the Sioux might resort to violence to fulfill the apocalyptic vision of the Ghost Dance. The issue came to a head at Pine Ridge in December of 1890 along Wounded Knee Creek. Following a now common practice, local officials responded to the popularity of the Ghost Dance by massing federal troops around the Sioux camps. Taken aback by the government's nervous reaction, the Ghost Dancers and their sympathizers withdrew to isolated areas and considered a response. They feared a white attack and wore Ghost Shirts that supposedly would turn away the soldiers' bullets. Believing Sitting Bull guilty of inciting the Ghost Dance, white authorities ordered Indian police to arrest him. When Sitting Bull resisted, he was killed. A group of armed dancers fled to the Badlands, where troops surrounded them at an encampment along Wounded Knee Creek. With four rapid-firing Hotchkiss guns trained on them, the Indians were surrendering their weapons on December 29 when a shot rang out. The resulting melee turned into a massacre that claimed the lives of 25 soldiers and about 200 Sioux men, women, and children.

As the Ghost Dance ebbed after the Wounded Knee tragedy, a new form of worship arose on the southern Plains. For centuries, the Indians of the lower Rio Grande Valley had ingested the crown of the peyote plant, a small, spineless cactus. Peyote, a hallucinogen, became central to a ritual for healing, prophesying, and acquiring spirit power. The Comanche had learned of peyote from the Apache decades before the reservation era. But construction of a railroad north from Texas during the 1880s allowed the plant to be imported into the Indian Territory in bulk. Incorporating aspects of

This Kiowa Ghost Dance dress was made from buckskin and decorated with traditional moon and star elements. The Ghost Dance started among the Kiowa in 1890, about the same time that the Sun Dance was outlawed.

A THRIVING TRADITION OF ART

Between 1870 and 1940, while anthropologists predicted the demise of traditional Indian culture, native arts nevertheless continued to thrive and evolve, reflecting reservation life and modern influences. Traditional crafts such as beadwork and basket making flourished, often incorporating new design motifs like the American flag. New skills, such as quilting, were taken up. New materials, including coins and even tin cans, were used to decorate clothing, much as elk teeth, dentalium shells, and deer hoofs had been used in the past. Objects new to the Indians, parasols and sunbonnets for instance, were decorated in traditional ways.

When growing numbers of white buyers expressed interest in collecting such creations, arts and crafts became an important source of income for the often impoverished reservation Indians. Their ability to adapt—to preserve much of the old and incorporate elements of the new—attests to the inventiveness of the Indian creative spirit. This ingenuity has been a hallmark of Indian culture since the time the first Athapaskans arrived in the Southwest from the subarctic forests and began to make useful household items from a material previously unknown to them—sunbaked clay.

The Hidatsa craftsman who made this drum sometime after 1920 maintained the ancient drum maker's tradition of painting powerful symbols on his handiwork—in this case, the American eagle on a shield of stars and stripes, relatively new images to the Hidatsa.

The abstract floral design adorning this Plains buckskin parasol was worked in glass beads and dyed porcupine quills and is known as Eastern Sioux style, which is said to reflect the influence of French fur traders. The black netting around the edges would have helped to cut the sun's glare.

The beaded American flags on this Ojibwa bandoleer bag contain four stars each, four being a sacred number to the Ojibwa and many other tribes. American flags became a popular motif among Indian artisans and their customers, but the extremely fine beadwork on this bag indicates that it was made for personal use rather than for sale.

Rows of shiny coins add flash and music to this cotton blouse (above) from the Winnebago Reservation in Nebraska. Coins were often appreciated as much for their decorative qualities as for their monetary value.

This small bag, made to be worn on a woman's belt, is beaded in a traditional Flathead style, with the non-traditional beaded elephant added in an overlay stitch.

The Sioux woman who wore this bonnet (left) probably appreciated its practicality in the hot sun, but could not resist the temptation to relieve its plainness with a band of beadwork.

It was not unusual for Indian men to borrow elements of Anglo-style clothing, such as military epaulets or stovepipe hats, but the Flathead woman who beaded this necktie and collar (left) about 1920 elevated the regimental stripe to a uniquely Indian work of art.

Jicarilla Apache basket makers learned to weave cylindrical baskets with handles and lids to sell as laundry hampers to white farm families. The diamond pattern integrated into the weave was typically Apache.

Christianity, the Peyote Road became a new religion that helped the people find relief from the degradations of their new life on the Comanche and Kiowa reservation and beyond. Despite attempts to ban it, by the end of the century, Indians on at least 16 reservations had embraced the movement, which later evolved into the modern Native American Church.

The Crazy Dogs, a Blackfeet religious society, perform the Medicine Lodge Dance, a part of the Sun Dance, on July 4, 1907. Indians used the occasion of American holidays, which they were encouraged to observe as part of the assimilation process, to celebrate their own traditions, including, sometimes, those that the government had banned.

The federal government took every opportunity to shrink the reservations. Under constant pressure from land-hungry settlers, railroads, and mining companies, officials pushed the tribes for further cessions and seized upon those rare instances of armed rebellion to appropriate and sell off tribal homelands. The earliest major uprising, by the Dakota in 1862, cost the Eastern Sioux their home reservations in Minnesota; they were scattered afterward to reservations in the Dakota Territory and Nebraska. The Dakota uprising also cost the neighboring Winnebago their reservation, although they had not taken part in the rebellion. And the Ute, as a result of their short-lived rebellion in 1879, lost mineral-rich holdings around the White River Reservation in western Colorado and were banished to a much smaller site in Utah.

Reduction of the largest reservation of all—the Great Sioux Reservation in South Dakota—resulted from a more complex chain of events. In

1874 a colonel named George Armstrong Custer led an expedition of cavalry and prospectors into the Black Hills in the western part of the reservation and announced the discovery of gold. As white miners flooded in, the government tried to purchase the region. The Sioux, who regard the Black Hills as sacred, refused to sell. Troops moved in to protect the miners, setting the stage for the storied defeat of Custer and his 7th U.S. Cavalry Regiment at the Little Bighorn in 1876. Three months later, officials imposed a fraudulent treaty upon the Sioux that forced them to cede the western third of the reservation, which included the Black Hills. In 1889 another government-imposed agreement fragmented the reservation. The remaining land was divided up into six separate agencies, and a 50-mile-wide corridor allocated for white use was opened all the way across the region.

The government meanwhile had been experimenting with another means of cutting back on Indian holdings. Known as allotment in severalty, this process broke up the reservation by distributing parcels of the land to individual Indian families, who would then hold ownership instead of the tribe. Since the typical reservation consisted of more than enough land to provide a substantial homestead for every family, allotment tended to produce a surplus of property, which could then be sold to whites. Throughout the 1800s, allotment had been tested extensively. Over the

Preparing for the Sun Dance, three Blackfeet women kneel before a buffalo skull and sweat lodge in 1945. They are sacramentally preparing the sacred buffalo tongues, stored inside the parfleche container in front of them.

preceding half-century, some 60 treaties had been signed to provide for parceling out tribal land to individuals. It had proved a windfall for whites, who not only bought up the land declared surplus but also gained control of most of the allotment parcels. Typical was the experience of the Ojibwa, who were granted 1,735 allotments in 1871. Seven years later, only one parcel in six was still in Ojibwa hands; the rest had passed to whites through fraud or sale at a fraction of their value.

Toward the end of the century, allotment would become comprehensive and compulsory for almost all of the Indians—a notion that possessed great appeal for reformers. In increasing numbers, well-meaning whites considered allotment the missing link in the Americanization of the Indians. All the elements previously considered essential to assimilation seemed to be falling short of their goals: Tribal structure remained strong, comparatively few Indians were farming, young and old alike resisted education, and Christianity had failed to attract converts in substantial numbers. The reservation—far from preparing the way for absorption of the Indian into mainstream America—actually had helped prevent it by developing into a stronghold of traditional customs and values.

Many reformers came to believe that the reservation itself had to be

With American flags flying from their canoes, a group of Tlingits approach the shore at Sitka, Alaska, to attend a potlatch in 1904. Although potlatching was outlawed in 1895, Pacific Northwest Indians secretly continued the tradition, often under the guise of celebrating American holidays.

Three Coast Salish initiates of the outlawed Spirit Dance wear their regalia in British Columbia about 1920. As prohibitions against traditional religion eased, the ceremony, which helps an individual gain spirit power, enjoyed a resurgence that continues today.

destroyed. Indians, they said, could never develop traits of individual enterprise until tribal ownership was abolished and each Indian family had its own homestead. Communalism was the key to the survival of the old ways, selfishness the key to civilization. "To bring him out of savagery into citizenship," Merrill Gates, the president of Amherst College, declared: "We must make the Indian more intelligently selfish before we can make him unselfishly intelligent. We need to awaken in him wants."

Congress approved the General Allotment Act in 1887. Known as the Dawes Act for its writer, Senator Henry L. Dawes of Massachusetts, the law authorized the president to partition the reservations and assign the resulting parcels to individual Indians—160 acres to each head of family and lesser amounts to single adults, minors, and orphans. Allotments could be doubled in areas where the land was suitable only for cattle raising. To prevent hasty sale of the land, title to each parcel was to be held in trust by the government for 25 years before being handed over. The Dawes Act contained other measures of far-reaching consequence. Acreage left over after allotment could be purchased by the government with tribal consent and the proceeds held in the U.S. Treasury for use by tribal members for "education and civilization." Upon receiving an allotment, the Indian became a citizen of the United States and subject to its laws and those of the state or territory. The law exempted from allotment about a dozen tribes for various reasons, including previous treaty provisions. Others, such as the Navajo and Apache in the arid Southwest, were effectively excluded because the law applied only to land promising for agricultural development.

Indians generally reacted to the allotment idea with a mixture of curiosity, outrage, and fear. Some felt that attaining individual deeds to land was their only protection against the inroads of whites. "I want a title to my land," said an Omaha farmer named Xitha Gaxe in a plea to Congress supporting allotment. "I want a house that is my own." But most saw the new law as the worst threat yet to Indian social and political identity. Ely

Parker, the Seneca Indian who served as President Grant's first commissioner of Indian affairs, favored assimilation but denounced the "red hot zeal" he observed among white legislators for the Dawes Act. "The Indians as a body are deadly opposed to the scheme," he reported, "for they see too plainly the certain and speedy dissolution of their tribal and national organizations." Some angry Indians resorted to sabotage when the surveying teams arrived. In Washington State, Yakimas tore out the boundary markers; in Wyoming, Northern Arapahos rode their mounts hell-for-leather through the surveyors' measuring tapes.

Indians understood most of all that allotment was simply a new kind of land-grab. The provision for government purchase of surplus holdings meant that much communal property, including ancestral burial sites and other places of sacred significance, would be lost. The first reservation to be surveyed and broken up, which belonged to the Iowa in the north-central Indian Territory, confirmed their worst fears. After each family received its 160-acre plot, some 90 percent of the reservation remained as surplus. The government snapped it up at nominal prices for granting to white homesteaders.

As for the individual allotment, the idea that a plot of his own would transform the Indian into a self-sufficient entrepreneur quickly proved unrealistic. Few Indians with the will to farm possessed the capital or experience. They had to have plows, draft animals, and seed, and government appropriations came nowhere near meeting the need; during the first 12 years after the Dawes Act, funds for such items averaged little more than a penny per acre of allotted land. Other allottees could not farm because they were too old, too young, physically disabled, or away at boarding school.

Attempting to deal with such problems, Congress in 1891 approved an amendment to the Dawes Act permitting Indians to lease their allotments to others. The response was swift on the Omaha and Winnebago reservations in Nebraska, which promoters of allotment had regarded as model locations for Indian farming. As soon as they could lease, residents stopped farming altogether to live off the small income they gained by

In a 1922 letter to residents of the Fort Berthold Reservation, agent Ernest Jermark sets down rules governing dancing. All festivities had to end by 2:00 a.m., and men under the age of 21 and women younger than 18 were not allowed to participate.

This drawing of a Hidatsa Grass Dancer (opposite), made in 1914, shows the distinctive bustle of a feather trail dancer, one of four honored officers of the dance. Hidatsa men learned the Grass Dance from the Sioux and adopted it as a means of culturally continuing their warrior identity.

An 1879 handbill advertises the availability for white settlement of previously protected Indian lands in the Kansas Territory. It predicts that more than 50,000 settlers will claim this land within 90 days.

renting their lands. A year after leasing became legal, 90 percent of the Indians on both reservations had rented all or part of their parcels to whites. Allotment, as President Theodore Roosevelt referred to it, was a "mighty pulverizing engine to break up the tribal mass."

The Indian Territory became a prime target for allotment. Railroads wanted the land along the right of way; mining corporations were eager to exploit coal, oil, and gas reserves. Prospective homesteaders camped on the borders in colonies of so-called Sooners and occasionally tried to squat on Indian lands. A preview of the intense pressure for allotment came when the government threw open to settlement the unassigned lands, two million unoccupied acres in the heart of the Indian Territory purchased from the Five Civilized Tribes. At a blast of the bugle at noon on April 22, 1889, some 50,000 Sooners rushed in to stake claims.

The government formally designated this region of settlement as the Oklahoma Territory the following year and stepped up the pressure on the surrounding reservations to submit to allotment and sale of surplus lands. In this process, replete with pitfalls, few tribes enjoyed the savvy and good fortune of the Quapaw. The Quapaw had a 56,000-acre reserve in the northern part of the Indian Territory. When federal officials proposed giving each Quapaw only 80 acres, the tribal leaders refused and organized their own allotment program. In 1893 the tribe allotted 200 acres to each of its members. Two years later, Congress approved this action, allowing the Quapaw to become the only tribe as yet to carry out their own allotment— and on lands where rich lead and zinc deposits would soon be discovered.

In the more typical allotment story, federal officials resorted to intimidation and chicanery when a tribe resisted. One of the longest struggles to stave off allotment was waged by the Comanche and the Kiowa. Under the terms of the Treaty of Medicine Lodge, which had created their joint reservation in the southwestern Indian Territory in 1867, any further land cession had to be approved by three-fourths of the adult males in the tribes. In 1892, by using every trick in their book, including the agent George Day falsely certifying that the agreement had the necessary signatures, federal commissioners managed to gain approval of allotment and its sale of surplus land. The two tribes held off ratification by Congress for eight years through the influence of Quanah Parker and other tribal leaders and lobbying by Texas cattlemen eager to retain their grazing leases. Even though Congress knew that the Indians had been tricked, in 1900, it approved the allotment anyway. The eventual sale of surplus lands claimed all but about 10 percent of the tribal holdings.

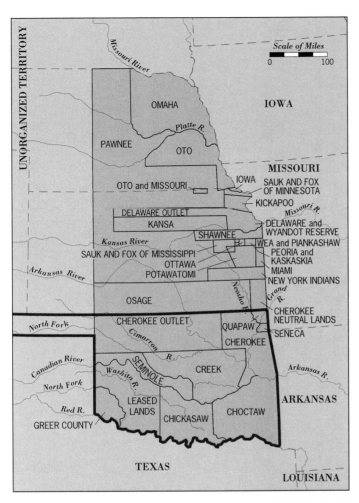

By 1854, after decades of Indian removal from the eastern United States, the Indian Territory that had been established in 1825 by President James Monroe along the western frontier of the United States had become a "protected" home to a host of Indian peoples (above). But the Kansas-Nebraska Act of 1854, enacted to make room for white settlement, called for the further division of the territory; the top half was reclaimed by the government and organized into the Kansas and Nebraska Territories, leaving only the bottom half for Indians.

Kiowa principal chief Lone Wolf sued the secretary of the interior and other officials on the basis of the Medicine Lodge treaty, contending that taking of tribal land violated the provisions requiring tribal approval. In 1903 in *Lone Wolf v. Hitchcock*, the Supreme Court not only ruled against the chief but undercut a century of treaty making. Congress, said the Court, had absolute power to regulate Indian affairs even if it meant abrogating a treaty. This clearly meant, as the commissioner of Indian affairs reported later, that land could be disposed of without the consent of the Indians. Backed by this new authority, officials rushed ahead with allotment for the Crow, Sioux, Ute, Northern Shoshone, and Flathead.

In the eastern part of the Indian Territory, meanwhile, federal commissioners focused on the nearly 20 million acres belonging to the Cherokee, Chickasaw, Choctaw, Creek, and Seminole, tribes who had been exempted from the Dawes Act largely because the permanent delegations that they maintained in

As white expansion pressed westward, more Indians were relocated to the Indian Territory. By 1879 the territory had been reduced to an area somewhat smaller than modern-day Oklahoma, and the number of tribes sharing this land had increased to 31 (right).

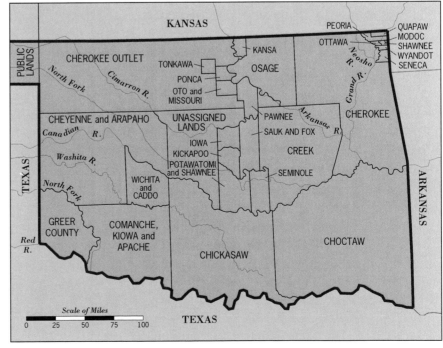

Washington lobbied effectively against it with Congress. Here were the Indians who had made the most progress toward white standards of civilization. Their school systems were producing more college graduates than the state of Texas. None of this could stop the allotment juggernaut.

Pressure to lift their exemption mounted. In 1890, after a presidential proclamation threatened to cut off their income from cattle-grazing leases, Cherokees agreed to sell part of the largely unoccupied Cherokee Outlet in the northwestern Indian Territory. The government added these six million acres to the new Oklahoma Territory and opened them to the greatest of the land rushes, when 100,000 whites stormed in to stake claims. In 1893 Congress decided to end the Five Civilized Tribes' exemption and authorized federal commissioners to begin negotiations for allotment. In 1898, after only two of the five groups had come to terms, Congress abolished their tribal governments and summarily ordered allotment. Ironically, so many allotments were granted—101,000, including those given to former slaves of the Five Civilized Tribes and whites married to tribal members—that very little surplus remained for sale to the government.

As the surveyors marked off the remaining lands, the Indians tried two last-ditch efforts to preserve their tribal governments. In 1901 a Creek named Chitto Harjo, also known as Crazy Snake, formed his own rump government and was jailed for insurrection. Later, in what became known as the Snake Uprising, he led hundreds of supporters into the back country but was eventually hunted down by federal troops and imprisoned.

In 1905 leaders of the five tribes drew up a constitution for converting the eastern part of the Indian Territory into an Indian state, to be named Sequoya in honor of the inventor of the Cherokee syllabary. The idea was overwhelmingly approved by Indian voters. Congress, however, preferred another solution: the merger of the shrinking Indian Territory into a single state—Oklahoma. Established in 1907, it took its name from the Choctaw phrase meaning "home of the red people."

By this time, most of the Indians in Oklahoma and elsewhere were surrounded by whites. Indian lands and resources were looked upon as commodities to buy or lease. Indian ways had been debased or outlawed, and many Indian leaders had been killed. Yet the reservation experience had failed to steal that which made the Indians distinct. Thanks to the inventiveness, strength, and obstinate endurance of their communities, the threads of memory that bound them to the past remained unbroken. Although their societies had been greatly altered, the kernels of their culture had survived the era of forced assimilation. ✛

The Kiowa Lone Wolf (seated, left), photographed with a Kiowa delegation to Washington, D.C., sued the U.S. government in 1901 to keep his people's lands intact. But the Supreme Court ruled that Congress had the right to abrogate treaties and reappropriate Indian lands.

HEAD, HAND, AND HEART

About midnight on April 13, 1878, a new group of students arrived at the Hampton Normal and Agricultural Institute in Virginia to begin their formal education. The hour was unusual but no more so than the students themselves, for the group consisted of Indians recently released from detention at Fort Marion in Florida. As prisoners taken in the aftermath of the Red River War, the Indians had received some basic instruction at Fort Marion under the supervision of their warden, U.S. Army captain Richard Henry Pratt. At the end of their three-year confinement, 17 men, mostly Cheyennes and Kiowas, opted to learn more about the "white man's road." Upon entering Hampton, they became the first Indians to attend an off-reservation boarding school.

Samuel Chapman Armstrong, who founded Hampton Institute as a school for freed slaves, was the only educator to answer Pratt's appeal to enroll the Indians. The son of missionaries and a former Union general in charge of black troops, Armstrong felt strongly that minorities should be educated according to the same standards as whites. Unlike Captain Pratt, however, who went on to establish the Carlisle Indian Industrial School and tried to assimilate Indians thoroughly into the main-

stream, Armstrong and the staff at Hampton did not wish to obliterate the students' cultural identity. Hampton's educators wanted their Indian graduates to return to the reservations with new knowledge and skills and impart them to others. Through a program of training "the head, the hand, and the heart"—academic knowledge, practical skills, and Christianity—Armstrong hoped to save Indians without sacrificing their heritage.

Some six months after the first students arrived, Armstrong expanded the program and accepted a second group. For the following 34 years, Congress helped pay for Indian education at Hampton Institute, supplying $167 (later $150) for each of 120 students every year. Controversial throughout its existence, Hampton's program was criticized for letting students "return to the blanket"—that is, resume tribal life. But when Congress withdrew federal funding in 1912, the deciding factor was blatant prejudice; one congressman from Texas demanded, "Why humiliate the Indian boys and girls, our wards and dependents, by educating them in the same school with Negro children?" Hampton kept educating Indians, however, by relying on private donations until 1923, when its last Indian student graduated.

Wigwam, Hampton's dormitory for Indian men, housed up to 100 students. As part of their training, Wigwam residents cleaned and maintained the premises, subject to daily inspections.

Fresh from the Dakota Territory, some still in native attire, Hampton's second group of Indian students assemble for their portrait in the fall of 1878. Richard Henry Pratt (center, top) recruited the 49 students from their reservation homes.

A Lakota Sioux student gave this brass-and-wood hair ornament to a Hampton teacher. The school's dress code, including regulation haircut and uniform, left no room for such adornments.

John Tiaokasin and his wife, Rosa Pleets, enrolled in the married students' program in 1887. Their first son, Richard (Young Eagle), was born at the school.

A UNIQUE EDUCATIONAL ENVIRONMENT

Hampton Institute, situated just 35 miles from Jamestown, where the first black slaves had been brought ashore, was established to train former slaves to be teachers and farmers. When the second group of Indian students arrived from the Dakota Territory, they asked to be housed with the black students, the better to learn English and new customs. School officials were concerned about conflict between the two groups, however, and relegated them to separate dormitories and dining halls. With some exceptions, Indian students also attended separate classes, where they learned the fundamentals. The result was an Indian department that one teacher called a "school within a school." Indians and blacks sometimes mingled on social occasions, however, and after 10 years, Samuel Armstrong could boast that the two groups had co-existed without a "single fracas."

After Armstrong's death in 1893, the emphasis at Hampton shifted from basic skills to more rigorous vocational instruction. Admission standards were raised, and new students entered Hampton with a stronger grasp of the fundamentals. In 1901 Hampton abandoned the Indian department, and thereafter black and Indian students attended classes together while Hampton's staff worked to preserve the cultural identity of both groups. Although the mingling of races did not seem to be a problem for the students, it was for some members of Congress, and the issue contributed to the loss of federal funding for the Indian students.

Louis Firetail, a Crow Creek Sioux, models tribal clothing for the students of his American history class in 1900. Hampton's on-campus museum displayed artifacts from cultures throughout the world, including the various Indian tribes, to encourage mutual respect.

This Sioux war bonnet, beautifully crafted of glass beads and eagle feathers on a felt-and-rawhide band, exemplifies the tribal handiwork exhibited in Hampton's museum.

Hampton's courses in domestic science, such as this nutrition class, went well beyond the basics. Students studying laundering, for example, learned how soap was made.

FORMING HABITS OF INDUSTRY

Although Hampton's curriculum did not neglect the head and the heart, training for the hand, or vocational instruction, took place in all settings—classrooms, workshops, farms, and dormitories. During the school year, the students worked to sustain the community. The men grew the food—a departure from the usual tribal custom of relegating planting to women—and helped erect and maintain the buildings. In Hampton's workshops, they made bricks, shoes, furniture, tinware, wagon wheels, and harnesses; they also ran a printing press and a sawmill. The women handled the cooking, cleaning, tailoring, dairying, and poultry raising—and mastered enough carpentry to manage a frontier homestead.

In addition, many students spent their summers in New England, living with white families and working for them to improve their English and earn money for their further education. As one faculty member put it, these outings were meant to "form habits of industry, promptitude, accuracy, and self-help."

Students in a dressmaking class conduct a fitting, convert measurements to a pattern, and sew the pieces on a machine. Women at Hampton made, mended, washed, and ironed not only their own clothing but also the mens' military-style uniforms as well.

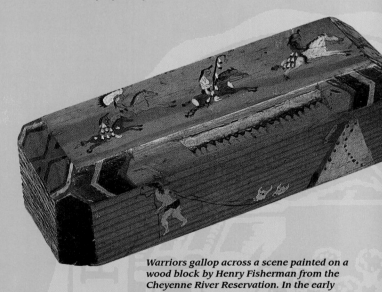

Warriors gallop across a scene painted on a wood block by Henry Fisherman from the Cheyenne River Reservation. In the early years, Hampton encouraged students to make and sell art to bolster self-sufficiency.

With farming tools in hand, Hampton students pose at Whipple Farm. Men learned agriculture by working at this on-campus farm and two other school-owned farms nearby, raising produce needed to feed the school's residents.

A teacher at Hampton demonstrates a method of separating cream as part of a dairying course designed to supplement the practical lessons of farming.

BEYOND SCHOOLING

As part of what one graduate called their "general upbuilding," Indians at Hampton engaged in many extracurricular activities. In the sitting rooms of the dormitories, students met for an evening conversation hour and participated in debates and contests. Many did community work with service organizations such as the Christian Endeavor Society and the Lend-A-Hand Club.

Some students played in the Wigwam Orchestra, and others sang in choruses or in the choir of a nearby Episcopal church. Sports for the men included baseball, basketball, football, and track; women students took up croquet, sailing, basketball, and gymnastics.

Although many of these activities were patterned after those at white schools, Indians took the new interests and skills they acquired at Hampton back home and enhanced tribal culture.

Hampton's all-Indian baseball teams, like the one portrayed above in the 1880s, played against local white clubs, an opportunity denied to black students. Later, Indians and blacks were integrated on Hampton's teams.

George Banks and John Badger, displaying Hampton's leafy insignia on their caps, played in a Crow Creek Agency brass band after leaving school. Skill with musical instruments was one of the many talents students took home with them.

Students portray figures from American history (left) in "Columbia's Roll Call," a pageant staged on Indian Citizenship Day, February 8, 1892. The celebration marked passage of the 1887 Dawes Act, which granted citizenship to Indian landowners.

"Talks and Thoughts," the Hampton Indian student newspaper, was published from 1886 to 1907. The motto, "Come over and help us," which appears on the masthead in both English and Sioux, was derived from the seal of the Massachusetts Bay Colony.

TALKS and THOUGHTS
OF THE
Hampton Indian Students
"Tahenan upi qa ounkiya hiye.—Come over and help us."

VOL. I. NO. 5.   HAMPTON, VA., MAY, 1886.   25cts. Per Year.

My Early School-Life.

My early school-life was done by compelling or whipping. When I first attend a day school, which was about two miles from where we live, and often times on cold days, I went to school, crying all the way to the school house, that this will do us good; because she never go to school herself. She used to get up early in the morning and got our breakfast ready and then woke us, washed our faces and combed our tangled hair, as we did not know how to take care of ourselves yet, and then sent us off. After we are gone, she will be off looking for, or feeding the ponies and do all the necessary works herself till we got home from school, which was out late in the afternoon. Well, soon as the school is out, my brother (who used to go to school here) and I, ran home just as fast as we could, see who will get home first, because the one that gets home first always have the best part of the dinner, but I am sorry to say that I am always left out, because I cannot run so fast as he could. Well soon as I see that he beat me, I stopped and cried, but that did not prevent him from getting the best part of the meal. I don't care very much in summer time, because there are lots of plums around the house, and I always satisfied myself by filling all my pockets full and be eating all the way home.

Then about our studies; we did not have very many things to study as we have now. The first thing we have to learn is the Dakota Alphabet, and after we have learned them thoroughly well, then we are taught to read in a higher book, which is the Bible. When we got in that class, we think we know everything, and don't care much about going to school any more. But after we have learned to read thoroughly well in our language, our mother sent us to a boarding school, which is fifteen miles below where

we live. But as we never have been away from our home before, we ran away the day after she took us there. We walked all the way home, but soon as she got home, she took us back again, but before she came away, / ran away and she got on a pony and chased me all over the prairie, till at last I got so tired, that I ran into a ditch and laid there for quite a while, feeling quite sure that I am out of the ditch and gave me a good whipping, and took me back to the school. I was a good boy after this. I never attempted to run away again, I stayed there six years, never even try to go home on vacations, till I was sent to another school (Riverside Institute, Lyons, Ia.,) where I stayed ten months, and then wrote back to the Bishop, telling him, that I would like to go home awful bad. What do you think that I want go home for? Well, I will tell you the reason; it is not a good reason at all; it was on vacation, and the principal of the school told me that I have to work for my board from 9 till 12 o'clock. But I told him that I don't care much about working here. "Well," he says, "You have to work for your living when you get home." "No, I don't have to work for my living, but I think I have said to him." I will make my living by drawing rations, but as soon as I got home, I have to work for my board also, and I did not depend on the rations any more. I often felt ashamed of what I have said about *living on rations*, and I try not to have any more of this kind or thoughts in my mind. And I advise all my Indian school-mates, not to depend on the rations, but work and make your own living.

Your friend,
ALEX. H. ESTES.
(*Sioux Tribe.*)

HAMPTON'S NOTABLE ALUMNI

Among the Indians who attended Hampton Normal and Agricultural Institute were the three students featured on these and the following pages—students whose diverse talents and substantial achievements left indelible impressions on the school and on their tribal communities. One of them was James Bear's Heart, a Cheyenne artist whose drawings dramatically represent the Plains Indians' way of life. Bear's Heart was in the first group of Indians at Hampton—17 inmates released from a Florida prison, where they were being held for participating in a rebellion in the West, and taken to the school in the spring of 1878. Bear's Heart studied English, mathematics, and the school's other academic subjects. He excelled in the classes teaching practical skills, such as carpentry, and earned the praise of his teachers for being remarkably "industrious" and "earnest." He worked long hours on Hampton's farms and during the summer outings, when he and the other students spent months living with white families and doing chores on their farms. When Hampton's second group of Indian students—mostly young Sioux from the Dakota Territory—arrived

in the fall of 1878, Bear's Heart worked hard to make the newcomers feel at home. By 1880 his English was so fluent that he was selected to deliver a speech at Hampton's 12th anniversary celebration.

Most of all, Bear's Heart matured as an accomplished artist and a skilled draftsman as he continued to produce works in the ledger-book style. Several samples are preserved in Hampton's own museum and in the collections of such museums as the Pennsylvania Academy of the Fine Arts and the National Museum of the American Indian.

Bear's Heart remained at Hampton Institute longer than any other member of the first group of Indians. He left in 1881, returning to live among his own people at the Cheyenne-Arapaho Agency at Darlington, in the Indian Territory. There his life took a turn for the worse. Shunned by some of his fellow Indians for his white ways, he struggled against poverty; subsequently, he became seriously ill with tuberculosis, the plague that claimed tragic numbers of Indian lives. He died the following year, in 1882, in his early thirties.

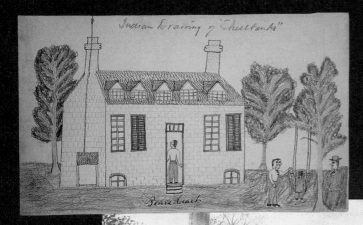

Bear's Heart's ink-and-pencil drawing (left) of the main building at Shell-banks—one of Hampton's farms—closely resembles the actual structure seen in the photograph below, which was taken about the same time. Bear's Heart enlivened his architectural drawings by including human figures.

A ceramic plate painted by Bear's Heart features a once familiar Plains scene—the buffalo hunt. Hampton's Indian students sold plates such as these to visitors and used the money to support themselves.

At left, wearing white men's clothes and holding rakes, spades, and other tools, members of Hampton's first Indian group sit for a photograph a few months after their arrival at the school. James Bear's Heart stands second from left in the back row.

Two mounted Indians in warrior's regalia gallop after a fleeing stallion in "Stealing Horses," one of Bear's Heart's depictions of tribal life, done in 1880 or 1881 for one of his teachers shortly before Bear's Heart left Hampton to return to the reservation.

A DOCTOR FOR HER PEOPLE

One of the most distinguished of Hampton Institute's early Indian graduates was Susan La Flesche, who became the first Indian woman licensed in the United States as a physician. Born in 1865, the daughter of an Omaha chief named Joseph La Flesche—or Iron Eyes—she first attended a small school on the Omaha Agency in eastern Nebraska, then traveled east to an academy for girls in Elizabeth, New Jersey, where she completed a three-year course of study in 1882.

Susan went east again in the fall of 1884 to attend Hampton. There she was salutatorian of her graduating class in 1886. She also became close friends with the school physician, Dr. Martha Waldron, who inspired her to move on to the Women's Medical College of Pennsylvania in Philadelphia. Again proving herself a superior student, Su-

san earned her degree after only three years of study in 1889.

Determined to help her own people, Susan returned to the Omaha Agency to set up practice. About this time she married Henry Picotte, a Yankton Sioux with whom she had two sons, Caryl and Pierre. She frequently worked 15-hour days, crisscrossing the agency in her horse-drawn buggy to visit the sick. Despite severe ailments caused by riding through freezing winter storms, she tirelessly served as the Omaha's translator, financial adviser, and Presbyterian missionary as well as doctor—and eventually raised the money to build a community hospital. Worn out finally by overwork and illness, she died at age 50 in 1915. Her last words were simply: "I am thankful I've been called and permitted to serve. I feel blessed for that privilege above all measure."

The hospital founded by Dr. Susan Picotte in 1913 stands on a hill in Walthill, Nebraska. Calling fresh air and sunshine "nature's medicine," she saw to it the building had a long, airy veranda for the patients.

An 1897 letter from Susan Picotte to an old Hampton friend describes her fondness for the institute, her life as a reservation doctor, and a recent near-fatal illness. "When I got well enough to go out," Picotte wrote, "I received so many congratulations from all, I felt so encouraged to try to do right and to live a better life."

Dressed in tribal clothing for a graduation day ceremony, Susan La Flesche stands in the middle of a group of Indian students that includes her future brother-in-law Charles Picotte (right), and to her right another notable Hampton woman, Anna Dawson.

THE PRECOCIOUS "LITTLE SISTER"

One of the youngest to enroll at Hampton and one of the first female Indian students to graduate, Anna Dawson, like Susan Picotte, was destined to become a pillar of her community. She arrived at age 10 in 1878 with the first group of Indians recruited from the Dakota Territory. She was accompanied by her widowed mother, Mary Dawson, who also became a student. A year and a half later, after returning to the reservation, her mother died of tuberculosis, and young Anna became a ward of the school as well as the favored little sister of the other students.

Graduating at age 16 in 1885, she taught at Hampton for two years before studying to be a teacher at Framingham Normal School in Massachusetts. After that graduation, she taught school among the Sioux in Nebraska, then once more returned east to study at the Boston YWCA. Gifted with a sharp intellect and unbridled curiosity, she enjoyed life in sophisticated Boston, becoming friends with a number of the city's Brahmins including Anna Longfellow, daughter of the famous poet. Then in 1895, Anna returned to her own people, the Arikara, serving for 17 years as a home economist on North Dakota's Fort Berthold Reservation. She married Byron Wilde, a graduate of the Carlisle Indian Industrial School, and they raised three adopted children while caring for many more. Tiny but indomitable, she remained a valued counselor to her tribe for the rest of her life, while over the years keeping in close touch with friends, fellow students, and teachers at Hampton. She died at age 100 in 1968.

Looking the part of a sophisticated easterner, Anna Dawson wears a high-necked dress, eyeglasses, and a severe hairdo in a studio portrait made about 1887 when she was a student in Framingham, Massachusetts.

Symbolic of her Indian heritage, the necklace Anna Dawson wore when she entered Hampton Institute consists of multicolored glass beads strung on cotton cloth. She gave the necklace to a Hampton faculty member, who donated it to the school's museum.

Having just arrived at Hampton Institute, Anna Dawson stands next to her mother, Mary, at far left in a group photograph of the nine original female Indian students, a group sent to the school from the Dakota Territory in 1878.

3

THE STRUGGLE FOR INDIAN RIGHTS

Turns Back Plenty, a line rider on the Crow Reservation in Montana, stands beside his car in this 1915 photograph. Line riders patrolled reservation borders, watching for trespassers and reporting breaks in the fences.

They were an eminent group by any measure. Physicians, lawyers, clergymen, writers, and social scientists—educated at America's best colleges and universities—some 50 of them from 18 different tribes gathered at a stately hotel in Columbus, Ohio, in the autumn of 1911. The symbolism of the city's name and of the date, October 12—the anniversary of Christopher Columbus's "discovery" of the New World—was not lost on the participants.

The occasion was the founding of the Society of American Indians. For the first time, Native Americans were coming together at the national level to promote the cause of all Indians. One of the group's founders, Arthur C. Parker, a prominent Seneca anthropologist, optimistically declared, "The Sioux is no longer a mere Sioux, or the Ojibwa a mere Ojibwa, the Iroquois a mere Iroquois."

Parker and his colleagues represented the educated elite of their people. Although some had been born on the reservation and spent a part of their childhood with their tribes, all had familial or other close ties to the white world. Prior to their years of higher learning, most of the society's founders had graduated from Carlisle and other Indian boarding schools. There they had survived homesickness and harsh regimentation to develop new skills and a sense of shared identity with Indians of other tribes. Now, in banding together to advocate education and other causes aimed at promoting Indian assimilation into white society, they also wanted to preserve what was uniquely Indian in their proud and diverse heritages.

These young activists, who came to be known as the Red Progressives, embodied a paradoxical turn in the lives of Native Americans during the early 20th century. It was a period of despair for many. Poverty, malnutrition, and disease were so prevalent that the Indian population had fallen below 250,000. Allotment was carving up reservations and undercutting tribal authority. And yet out of the wreckage of the reservation system arose a new assertiveness in politics, culture, and religion. Largely under the leadership of the Red Progressives, Indians revitalized old institutions

and invented new ones. Their formidable task was to somehow ease integration into the larger society without sacrificing their "Indian-ness."

The crowded agenda of the newly formed Society of American Indians reflected the new consciousness among educated Indians. The society established headquarters in Washington, D.C., to watch over new legislation and started publishing a quarterly journal, *American Indian Magazine.* One of the society's main priorities was promoting full citizenship for all Indians. It selected the American eagle as the society's official emblem and encouraged Indians to sing "The Star-Spangled Banner" at public gatherings. At the same time, it celebrated that which was uniquely Indian. The society publicized the exploits of Indian athletes such as the Sauk and Fox named Jim Thorpe, the Carlisle graduate who dominated the 1912 Olympics. The society sponsored Descendants of American Aborigines, an organization modeled after the Daughters of the American Revolution, and persuaded three states to observe American Indian Day on June 22—traditionally the time of the "moon of the first fruits."

The Society of American Indians became a valuable forum, allowing Indians from different backgrounds to share ideas and vent resentments. Its diversity was reflected in the personalities of two of the organization's founders: Charles Eastman and Carlos Montezuma. Both men had survived turbulent boyhoods, attended white colleges, married white women, and served as physicians on reservations. But they frequently stood far apart in their ideas.

Charles Eastman—Ohiyesa—was a best-selling author and the most prominent of the society's founders. He was a Dakota Sioux who, at the

Delegates to the 1913 annual meeting of the Society of American Indians gather for an official portrait at Wildcat Point outside Denver. Formed to assist Indian legal claims and promote reform of Indian affairs, the organization was the first to bring pan-Indian representatives together at the national level.

age of four, had seen his father, Many Lightnings, sent off to prison for his role in the Minnesota uprising of 1862. His grandmother had raised him, and although fiercely antiwhite, she had given him advice that carried him far: "When you see a new trail, or a footprint that you do not know, follow it to the point of knowing." As a physician at the Pine Ridge Agency in South Dakota, he had tended to the Lakotas wounded by soldiers at Wounded Knee in 1890. He was a moderate and a romantic, who seemed to move easily between the white world and the reservation. In his 10 books, he wrote of an idealized Indian past and tried, he said, "to emphasize its universal quality, its personal appeal."

Carlos Montezuma—Wassaja—was born a Yavapai-Apache in central Arizona in 1867. When he was four, the Apache's ancient enemies, the Pima, captured the boy and sold him for $30 to Carlos Gentile, a reporter and photographer of Mexican extraction. They traveled the United States

Members of the Society of American Indians, white associate members, and guests enjoy a banquet at the Hotel Walton in Philadelphia in February 1914. Seated at the table along the far wall are Indian and white dignitaries who addressed the distinguished gathering.

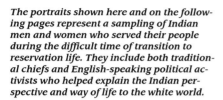

The portraits shown here and on the following pages represent a sampling of Indian men and women who served their people during the difficult time of transition to reservation life. They include both traditional chiefs and English-speaking political activists who helped explain the Indian perspective and way of life to the white world.

JOSEPH
Nez Percé

together, and Montezuma attended public schools. He worked his way through college and medical school. Service as a physician at Indian schools and on the reservation shaped his antigovernment views. In 1906 he refused an offer by President Theodore Roosevelt to head the Bureau of Indian Affairs and then launched a campaign to abolish the bureau and the reservations it administered.

Aggressively self-made, Montezuma argued that the bureau's paternalism prevented the Indian from progressing. Like Richard Pratt, the founder of the Carlisle school where Montezuma once worked, he believed in instant assimilation: "The best thing for the good of the Indian is to be thrown on the world. He must do it himself; it cannot be done for him." Increasingly vocal, he started his own monthly publication and openly lashed out at mainstream members of the society. "I can lick you," he yelled at a moderate leader during one public debate. "My tribe has licked your tribe before."

Widely known as the "fiery Apache," Montezuma became the most divisive force in the society. His intransigence weakened the organization's impact on public opinion and caused internal fractures. In 1922 Montezuma fell ill with diabetes and tuberculosis. He insisted on going back to the Arizona reservation where he was born to spend his last

GALL
Hunkpapa Sioux

WASHAKIE
Eastern Shoshone

months. There, in January 1923, he died in a wickiup attended by Yavapai-Apache medicine men. Not long afterward, the Society of American Indians also expired—but not before it had established an eloquent precedent in speaking out for Indian pride.

An issue that contributed to the society's demise was the controversy over the religion based on peyote. In 1915 a majority of delegates to the group's convention refused a plea to support the religion against threats of legal suppression from local, state, and federal authorities. The society, in fact, went on record in favor of federal legislation to outlaw the use of peyote. These votes split the membership, driving away peyote advocates.

The society's position baffled many Indians because the new religion, like the society itself, theoretically embraced all tribes and accommodated both the traditional and the new. Peyotists prescribed a strict code of personal behavior, including sobriety, monogamy, and emphasis on hard work and self-reliance. Many of the adherents were young Red Progressives, graduates of Indian boarding schools. They considered Peyotism the Indian religion, the Indian brand of Christianity. More and more elements of the Christian faith were integrated into Peyotism. Proponents reported that Jesus Christ appeared in their peyote-induced visions, and they likened the sacramental ingestion of a peyote button to the eucharistic use of bread

PLENTY COUPS
Crow

SARAH WINNEMUCCA
Northern Paiute

and wine. The new religion was spread by leaders called peyote roadmen who, like evangelists, went from tribe to tribe preaching the word.

The peyote cult, however, was a target for ardent critics. Both Indian traditionalists and Christian missionaries rejected Peyotism. The missionaries publicly denounced the cactus as a sinful, addictive drug—although no one could prove that eating a peyote button was habit forming—and expressed concern that the cult undermined their attempts to convert the Indians. Government officials worried that the cult diverted devotees from assimilation, leaving "the Indian contented with his present attainments" and cutting him off from "the possibility of healthful aspirations," as Robert G. Valentine, commissioner of Indian affairs, put it. Authorities were so determined to crush the cult that they banned James Mooney, a widely respected anthropologist and a defender of the right to use peyote, from conducting research on the Kiowa reservation.

To defend the new religion against governmental assaults, Peyotists borrowed from the ideals and institutions of white society. They emphasized not only its resemblance to Christianity but also the right to religious expression guaranteed by the U.S. Constitution. In 1918 the thousands of followers in Oklahoma legally incorporated as the Native American Church in order "to foster and promote the religious belief in the Christian

SHARP NOSE
Northern Arapaho

CARLOS MONTEZUMA
Yavapai-Apache

religion with the practice of the Peyote Sacrament and to teach morality, sobriety, industry, kindly charity, and right living." The new religion swept through the reservations so rapidly that by 1930 perhaps half of the nation's Indian population were members of the Native American Church.

Legends attesting to the mystical power of the new church sprang up. A Washoe leader from Nevada asserted that this new "medicine"—peyote—inspired a vision of important documents essential to the Washoe's fight for rights. In this vision, the documents resided in the archives in Washington, D.C. According to the legend, five tribal members went to the nation's capital in search of the papers. They found them, but federal officers chained the intruders and locked the door. "Them Indians are still there," the Washoe leader said. "Sometimes when you take the medicine and pray for them in a meeting, you can see them there. Some day I think Indians will go there and let them out. They will find the treaties of all the Indians. . . . When that day comes, the medicine will show us the next thing we must do."

Other forms of cultural expression blossomed on the reservation and found favor in the larger society. The Arapaho artist Carl Sweezy worked with butcher paper and house paint to depict sacred rituals and other scenes from tribal history. The watercolor, pencil, and ink renderings of the Shawnee artist Ernest Spybuck also drew the interest of art collectors.

RAIN IN THE FACE
Hunkpapa Sioux

GERTRUDE SIMMONS BONNIN
Yankton Sioux

Traditional dances diffused across tribal lines and began to attract the attention of white tourists. The Grass Dance, which had been performed only by Pawnee and Omaha warriors, was taken up by the Lakota Sioux and other Plains tribes, who also adopted the Omaha's traditional deer-hair head roaches and feather bustles.

A new generation of leaders emerged at the tribal level as well as nationally. Boarding school graduates returning home armed with a mastery of the English language and an understanding of American political and legal institutions used their knowledge to try to right old wrongs. In northern Wisconsin, Menominee opposition to federal control over the tribe's large timber reserves was led by Reginald Oshkosh, son of the traditional chief and a Carlisle graduate. In Washington State, Yakimas went into the federal courts in 1904 to successfully reaffirm tribal fishing rights that had been established by treaty. The Gros Ventre and the Assiniboin in 1908 won a decision from the U.S. Supreme Court ratifying their rights to water on the Fort Belknap Reservation in northern Montana. Patrick Miguel, son of a Yuma leader and a former Carlisle student, spoke for many in the new generation. Urging the commissioner of Indian affairs to hold tribal elections at the Fort Yuma reservation in Arizona, Miguel wrote, "We believe the old Indians should be taught more by members of

JOHN ROSS
Cherokee

SATANTA
Kiowa

their own tribe, in a kindly way, to see and adopt the white man's laws. . . ."

The most far-reaching legal offensive was launched by the Lakota. Nearly 100 official delegates from nine different Sioux communities met in 1911 on the Cheyenne River Reservation to form the Black Hills Treaty Council. The council's purpose was to develop a plan for prosecuting the Sioux claim that the United States had taken the Black Hills fraudulently in 1876. Delegates selected as their chairman a young boarding school graduate named James Crow Feather who epitomized the new breed of Red Progressives. In his tailored suit and black top hat, Crow Feather looked right at home when he ventured into the councils of white power, but the miniature tomahawk pinned in his lapel bespoke his Sioux identity.

Lakotas of all political persuasions rallied around the Black Hills Council. Together with other young Sioux leaders such as Henry Standing Bear, a Carlisle graduate and a key figure in the Society of American Indians, Crow Feather and the council plotted a legal strategy. They wanted to file suit in the U.S. Court of Claims but first needed congressional legislation to give that court jurisdiction to hear their grievances. In 1915 they drafted such a bill for consideration by Congress. To finance lobbying trips to Washington, the Indians staged reservation "singings" in which leaders chanted traditional songs of praise in return for donations.

HENRY CHEE DODGE
Navajo

RED CLOUD
Oglala Sioux

The necessary measure finally passed Congress in 1920. The following year, the council filed 24 lawsuits against the federal government seeking nearly $1 billion as compensation for the taking of the Black Hills, misappropriation of tribal funds, and other grievances. Although it took more than a half-century, the Sioux won in excess of $100 million in claims between 1974 and 1989. By then, dozens of other tribes had followed the trail blazed by the Sioux.

Another quest undertaken early in the 20th century was the attainment of U.S. citizenship for all native-born Indians. The process of conferring citizenship upon these first Americans was taking place at a grudging pace—via special treaties during the 19th century and through allotment and companion congressional acts such as the 1901 measure that made citizens of members of the Five Civilized Tribes. World War I hastened the process. More than 12,000 Indians volunteered to serve in the U.S. armed forces. Unlike blacks, who were segregated, the Indians served alongside whites in integrated units. Many Indians distinguished themselves, including the Choctaw Joseph Oklahombi, who won the French Croix de Guerre for single-handedly capturing 50 enemy machine guns and bringing in 171 German prisoners. After the war, citizenship was provided to returning Indian servicemen who did not already enjoy that privilege.

QUANAH PARKER
Comanche

Yet one-third of the Indians still were not American citizens. Groups such as the Iroquois confederacy of New York actually opposed citizenship as a threat to their professed status as sovereign nations. The Iroquois had insisted on making their own declaration of war against Germany during World War I and giving special authorization to their young men to serve in the American armed forces as "allies" of the United States. By 1924, when Congress formally conferred citizenship on all Indians, many considered it an empty gesture. Because states could establish their own election qualifications, citizenship did not even bring the right to vote; it would be 24 years before Indians could cast the ballot in every American state. The Sioux author Luther Standing Bear called citizenship the "greatest hoax ever perpetrated upon" the Indian.

Indeed, the enormous loss of Indian-owned land made citizenship seem hollow. The allotment process, launched in 1887 by the Dawes Act, gained momentum after the turn of the century. From 1900 to 1910, the amount of tribal land partitioned for allotments more than quadrupled. But the parcels allotted to individual Indians fell into white hands at an alarming rate. Although the Dawes Act dictated that each plot be held in trust by the federal government for 25 years after allotment to prevent sale of the property and thus keep it in Indian hands, a succession of amendments to the law allowed premature transfers of the land through lease or purchase.

Liberalized leasing policies, for example, encouraged the Cheyenne and Arapaho to rent out more than 85 percent of their allotted parcels to non-Indians by 1911. For many families, leasing their allotments became the main source of income. This rental income often proved insufficient, however, leading a prominent Arapaho, Cleaver Warden, Carlisle-educated peyote roadman, to favor allotment sales to alleviate poverty among his people. Restrictions on sale of allotted lands were designed to protect the allottee, but Warden argued that an Indian should be "treated like a white man and let him suffer the consequences if he does make a mistake."

Some laws did allow the sale of allotments held in trust under special circumstances. Allottees deemed too sick, too old, or otherwise "noncompetent" to develop their parcels could lease them with government permission. Sale was permitted when the death of the allottee left the parcel in the

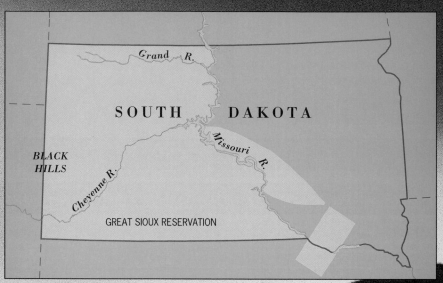

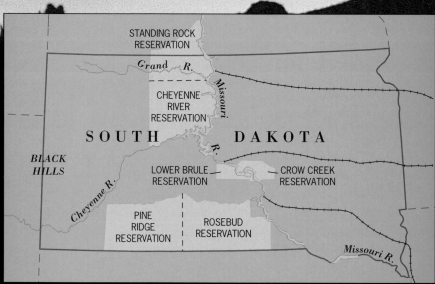

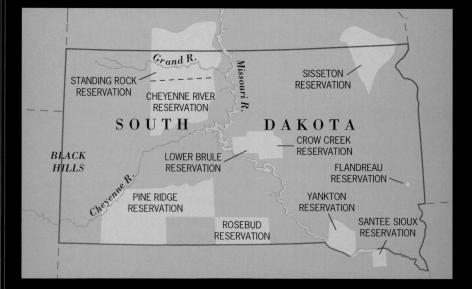

White commissioners and Lakota leaders—some of whom are shown in the photograph at right—established the Great Sioux Reservation at an 1868 treaty council at Fort Laramie. As part of the agreement, the U.S. government prohibited white settlers from entering the reservation (dark gray), shown in the map at top left. Twelve years after the passage of the Black Hills Act, Congress, intent on separating and confining the various Sioux bands, squeezed the Indians into smaller spaces—and out of the Black Hills (middle map). The bottom map reflects the various Sioux reservations of today.

A CLAIM FOR SACRED LANDS

To the Lakota, or Western Sioux, the Black Hills of South Dakota are the holiest place on earth. They call the 6,000-square-mile area the "heart of everything that is." Ever since the tribe migrated to the Plains from the woodlands of the upper Mississippi Valley, the ancient mountains have been the spiritual center of their universe. When the Lakota agreed to the treaty of 1868 at Fort Laramie, Wyoming, the Black Hills were included in the Great Sioux Reservation.

In 1874, when gold was discovered in the region, the federal government attempted to buy the Black Hills back. The idea of selling was inconceivable to the Sioux. So in 1877 Congress simply passed an act appropriating the land. In 1920 the Indians launched a series of legal counterattacks, challenging the confiscation and eventually winning in two different courts. Following a 1980 Supreme Court ruling, the Sioux turned down a cash settlement of about $106 million, a sum that has since grown to more than $400 million in an interest-bearing account. The Lakota people cannot be whole until they regain their sacred Black Hills; the final chapter in this saga remains to be written.

hands of more than one heir. Most Indians died without a will and left many heirs to share equally in the estate. Division of the land among them tended to fragment the holding, rendering it too small to be productive. Further subdivision through subsequent generations led to inheritances as tiny as a fraction of an acre. "There are pieces of land. . .so divided among heirs," wrote Ruth Muskrat Bronson, a Cherokee, "that the annual lease income therefrom to any one heir is less than one cent." The government hoped that proceeds from selling the land would enable heirs to improve their own allotments, but the effect was to turn over more land to white buyers.

The legislation that ultimately opened the floodgates for sale of allotments was the Burke Act of 1906. Sponsored by Charles Burke, a South Dakota congressman eager to make more Indian land available to white settlement, the measure provided a shortcut for the 25-year trust period. The secretary of the interior was empowered to issue title to an allotment "whenever he shall be satisfied that any Indian allottee is competent and capable of managing his or her affairs." Anyone could apply and, if deemed competent, could receive immediate title to the allotment and thus the right to sell the land. The government was so eager to grant approval that seven of every eight applicants—many of them applying at the behest of unscrupulous land speculators—were deemed competent in 1907. About 60 percent of those receiving titles during the first two years soon sold their allotments and squandered the proceeds. An Indian Bureau inspector, Edgar A. Allen, discovered that all but two of 97 of the "most promising allottees" among the Cheyenne and Arapaho had quickly sold out, most of them receiving far below market value. "The granting of these [titles]," he concluded, "brings joys to the grafter and confidence man and abject poverty to the Indian."

When applications lagged, so-called competency commissions from the Indian Bureau scoured the reservations in search of likely candidates. Members went from tipi to tipi, house to house, interviewing the occupants to see if they were sufficiently "civilized" to assume the responsibilities of outright ownership of their allotments. In attempting to elicit evidence of competence, they typically spent less than 15 minutes in such interviews, asking about the respondent's education, employment, and previous experience with whites. Even after being judged competent by the commission, some Indians refused to accept immediate ownership, preferring to leave their land under federal protection.

The Indian Bureau began forcing title upon reluctant allottees. To make the process more attractive, government officials staged elaborate pageants known as last-arrow ceremonies. The entire reservation would be invited to assemble before a large ceremonial tipi that contained the candidates for land titles who had been deemed competent. One by one, the candidates emerged from the lodge in traditional dress and armed with a bow and arrow. Each was ordered by the presiding government official to fire one last arrow, symbolizing his old Indian status. He then returned to the tipi and came back in citizen dress. The candidate then stood before a plow to symbolize his acceptance of the white man's road and received a purse and an American flag pin as tokens of his new status.

In order to speed up declarations of competence and catch those missed by the commissions, Indian affairs commissioner Cato Sells announced in 1917 a "policy of greater liberalism." Hailing the "beginning of the end of the Indian problem," Sells, a former Texas banker, declared that competence henceforth could be measured by blood and schooling. Adult Indians who possessed at least half white ancestry would receive immediate ownership of their allotments—whether they wanted it or not—along with their share of tribal money held in trust by the government. Those who had graduated from a government school also received title to their parcel after a brief competence interview.

More than 10,000 titles were granted during the next three years—and so many were thereupon sold to white bankers, businessmen, and farmers that Sells's successor suspended the new policy. The new commissioner noted in 1921 that, competent or not, more than two-thirds of all those who had received title prematurely had been "unable or unwilling to cope with the business acumen coupled with the selfishness and greed of the more competent whites, and in many instances have lost every acre they had." He reinstituted the practice of requiring formal application and proof of competence. This new commissioner was Charles Burke, the former congressman whose 1906 legislation had launched the whole process of granting titles prematurely.

When Burke took office in 1921, more than half the Indians in tribes affected by the Dawes Act were landless, and allotment would continue for more than another decade. Many of the original allotments still in Indian hands were being farmed by whites under lease. Intended ostensibly for the Indians' benefit to assure them protected homesteads where they could farm and become self-reliant, allotment instead pauperized most of them. The number of acres under cultivation actually had declined.

Standing beside a plow symbolic of his new life as a farmer, a Sioux resident of Standing Rock Reservation shoots the "last arrow" during an admission to citizenship ritual developed by the secretary of the interior in 1916. Other Sioux men holding arrows await their turn. Each new citizen received a purse (left), symbolic of thrift, and a pin (below), to be worn as a badge of patriotism. After being addressed by their Indian names one last time, the men were given a white name, stood before a plow, and listened to a lecture about the importance of work; the women received a workbag and a speech about a woman's role in the home.

Reservations resembled checkerboards, with leased and sold allotments interspersed among Indian-owned plots. These fragmented lands were unsuitable for grazing large cattle herds or for the large-scale cultivation that increasingly supplanted subsistence farming across America.

Allotted lands were most valuable—and vulnerable—in the state of Oklahoma, the former Indian Territory, which contained about one-third of the nation's Native Americans. These tracts drew special attention from whites because many of them featured, besides rich soil or lush grass, other exploitable resources such as dense forests, veins of coal, lead, and zinc, and the world's most extensive known petroleum deposits. Allotments for many of Oklahoma's multitude of tribes had been carried out under special legislation allowing fewer restrictions than the Dawes Act and its amendments—and more rapid loss of lands. For example, by 1924 well over half of the allotments granted the 101,209 enrolled members of the Five Civilized Tribes and their former black slaves had been transferred to white ownership, usually at prices below market value.

Allotments held by minors and adults deemed incompetent were susceptible to abuse under another special federal law for the Indians of Oklahoma. Matters of guardianship and probate were handled by county courts instead of the U.S. government. In many counties, serving as a guardian for Indians with lucrative allotments became a profitable profes-

A government allotment officer (center), assisted by an interpreter, takes information from American Horse, an Oglala Sioux leader, at Pine Ridge Reservation, South Dakota. Between 1904 and 1916, the 2,721,597-acre reservation was split up into 8,275 plots totaling 2,380,195 acres. The leftover land was either sold to the government or assigned to the tribe as a whole.

sion, often the sole occupation, for lawyers and others with connections at the courthouse. Corrupt judges allowed guardians to charge their wards scandalously high costs for handling oil royalties or other income from the property. One guardian had no fewer than 51 Indian children as wards, and some of them went homeless and hungry because of his malfeasance. Competition for control of Indian estates grew so fierce that some presumptive guardians committed perjury, forgery, kidnapping, and even murder to get hold of them.

The scandal gained national exposure in 1924 when the Indian Rights Association published a pamphlet with a title that spelled out the corruption in no uncertain terms: *Oklahoma's Poor Rich Indians: An Orgy of Graft and Exploitation of the Five Civilized Tribes—Legalized Robbery.* One of the authors was Gertrude Simmons Bonnin, a Yankton Sioux who had helped found the Society of American Indians and had established a kind of settlement house for the society on a reservation in Utah to help Utes improve their lives. The blunt-spoken Bonnin was one of those remarkable Red Progressives who emerged from the reservation early in the 20th century—a violinist, teacher, social reformer, and prolific writer of short stories and articles under the pen name Zitkala-sa.

The pamphlet, based on the authors' five-week investigation in eastern Oklahoma, lambasted judges, guardians, attorneys, bankers, and merchants—even undertakers—for collusion in the scandal. Indian estates, they wrote, were being "shamelessly and openly robbed in a scientific and ruthless manner." Judges permitted guardians and attorneys to collect

A Lakota father and son relax in front of their log-and-sod cabin on the Rosebud Reservation in South Dakota. When the weather was warm, the family slept in the nearby tipi. The dual dwellings can still be seen on Plains Indian reservations.

"unconscionable fees and commissions." Administrative costs ran as high as 70 percent of the value of an estate. Many of the victims described in the pamphlet were children, but the authors also cited instances of wealthy adults suddenly being taken under the avaricious wing of the court. "When oil is 'struck' on an Indian's property," they wrote, "it is usually considered prima facie evidence that he is incompetent, and in the appointment of a guardian for him his wishes in the matter are rarely considered."

Among the instances of "legalized plunder" described by Bonnin and her colleagues, perhaps the most poignant was that of a Choctaw girl. In 1921, when the town banker relied on guile to replace her uncle as legal guardian, Ledcie Stechi was seven years old. She owned 20 oil-producing acres inherited from her mother and had $2,000 in the bank from the sale

Blackfeet listen to a white agricultural expert explain how to raise wheat at the Blackfeet winter fair in Browning, Montana—an annual event organized by the Indian Office. The fair also provided an opportunity to socialize and display traditional crafts.

of some land. Nonetheless, Ledcie was forced to live in poverty with her aged grandmother because the guardian allowed them only a monthly credit of $15 for food. In two years she grew sick and emaciated. Her health improved after friendly whites gave her medical treatment, and she was placed in an Indian school. But her guardian immediately took her out of school, and one month later, she died in his custody. The grandmother was convinced he had poisoned her, but the guardian had the body buried before it could be examined. The grandmother inherited Ledcie's oil-rich land—and an unwanted guardian hastily appointed by the court.

The richest allotments belonged to the Osage. After being pushed around prairie and plains by the United States for much of the 19th century, the tribe had settled on an otherwise unremarkable reservation in present-day northern Oklahoma that happened to sit atop an underground ocean of oil. Although the full potential of petroleum was not yet apparent in the decade after the first big gusher was brought in at Bartlesville in 1897, the Osage showed great foresight. They won permission from Congress to execute their own allotment scheme in 1906, partitioning the 1.5-million-acre reservation so that each of the tribe's 2,229 members received four plots totaling just over 650 acres. The Osage reserved all subsurface mineral rights for the tribe as a whole, with the proceeds from oil leases and royalties to be divided evenly among tribal members.

Oil income burgeoned in the new era of the automobile, and by the 1920s, the Osage were the richest group of people in the world. At the peak of their affluence, in 1925, every man, woman, and child with a so-called headright—the equal share of oil rights given members at allotment in 1906—received an annuity of $13,400. This was an enormous sum in those days—the equivalent of more than one million dollars 70 years later—and numerous families had several headrights. Many Osages spent the money with such abandon that reporters descended on them to record such profligacies as $1,000-a-month grocery bills (at a time when steak sold for 25 cents a pound). They cruised over the dusty prairie roads in brand-new, chauffeur-driven Pierce-Arrow limousines with the owner's initials etched in solid gold on the side panels. Grand mansions sprouted among the forests of tall wooden oil derricks, although the owners, it was reported, often preferred to sleep outside on the lawn.

George Vaux Jr., chairman of the Board of Indian Commissioners, a group of advisers to the Indian Bureau, commented after a visit to Osage

County, Oklahoma, in 1920: "Their wealth literally has been thrust upon them, unwittingly on their part. They are almost, if not quite, dazed by it. . . .These people do not know what they are doing; they have never been trained, nor have they the opportunity to learn what it all means. That the money is being largely squandered is evident. Of course, a great deal of it goes into automobiles; many Osages have several, and they are all high-priced cars. One rarely sees an Osage in a Ford."

The sudden wealth of the Osage had a dark side. During the early 1920s, what came to be known as the reign of terror befell the tribe. Unscrupulous whites stopped at nothing, not even murder, in order to gain control of oil-rich Osage land. A wave of murders brought in agents from the Federal Bureau of Investigation (FBI), who discovered that the motives for the killings were elementary. Almost all of the murders involved Osages whose white guardians or white husbands would benefit by taking over the headright. It was common knowledge that a killer could be hired for $500 and a used roadster. The favorite modus operandi was to get the Osage drunk, find a doctor who would attest to this condition, and then later give the victim a lethal injection of morphine. Invariably the cause of death was said to be alcohol poisoning. By some estimates, up to 60 Osages were murdered, nearly three percent of the tribe, before the presence of the FBI and congressional legislation bringing guardians under control of the Indian Bureau helped stop the killing.

The Osage Guardianship Act as well as the exposé of Oklahoma's probate scandals resulted from a revival of public concern about the Indian during the 1920s. This interest arose largely through the efforts of a growing reform movement. Much of the movement consisted of the old-line reformers such as the Indian Rights Association and other public-spirited groups that had favored allotment and other policies aimed at assimilating Native Americans. Now they were joined by a cadre of white intellectuals, social scientists, and philanthropists eager not only to treat Indians humanely but also to preserve their lands and tribal heritage.

Reformers old and new coalesced around the threat to the historic land rights of the Pueblo Indians in the Southwest. These land rights, which dated back to grants made by the king of Spain during the 16th century, were recognized by the U.S. government when it acquired the region after the Mexican War. Unlike most other American Indians, the various Pueblo groups were granted citizenship and the right to do whatever they pleased with their lands, which were not regarded as reservations. Over the years, some land was acquired by non-Indians. Individual members volun-

tarily sold their property, and other tracts with valuable water rights were occupied by non-Indian squatters, whom the Pueblos were unable to expel.

A decision by the U.S. Supreme Court in 1913 altered this situation and set up the threat to the Pueblos. In the case, which actually tested the government's power to control alcohol, the Court reversed the longstanding legal status of the Pueblo communities. It ruled that their lands comprised reservations under the protection of the United States like those of other tribes. This meant that Pueblo land could not be transferred without the authorization of the federal government. The decision's most immediate impact was not on the Pueblos but on the 12,000 non-Indian neighbors who had settled there by purchasing property or simply by squatting on it. Their land claims were now in legal jeopardy.

In order to counter the possible expulsion of these New Mexicans, a U.S. senator from that state, Holm Bursum, introduced a controversial bill in 1922. His proposal would have placed upon the Pueblos the burden of proving ownership of their lands, thus virtually validating all non-Indian claims of title held for more than 10 years prior to 1912. These claims represented only about one-tenth of Pueblo lands but a much higher percentage of the precious irrigated tracts.

Late in 1922, 121 representatives from a score of different Pueblo communities gathered at Santo Domingo, New Mexico, for the All-Pueblo Council. It was the first time the highly independent Pueblos had come together against a common enemy since 1680, when they united to defeat the Spaniards. The Pueblo delegates issued an "appeal to the American

Members of a 1918 Osage wedding procession are attired in beaded, brilliantly colored feather hats and military-style coats like the ones at right. The discovery of oil on Osage land in 1894 provided families the wealth to afford elaborate wedding ceremonies.

people for fair play and justice and the preservation of our pueblo life." The Bursum Bill, they declared, "will destroy our common life and will rob us of everything which we hold dear—our lands, our customs, our traditions."

The council then launched a lobbying and publicity campaign. A delegation of elders traveled to Washington, D.C., and New York City carrying silver-topped canes that President Abraham Lincoln had given the Pueblos symbolizing their right to perpetual possession of their land. Back home, the Taos and Santa Fe colonies of white artists and writers rallied to the cause. A petition on behalf of the Pueblos bore the names of prominent writers such as Zane Grey, D. H. Lawrence, and Carl Sandburg. Lawrence, the English expatriate, asserted in a letter to the *New York Times* that the Bursum Bill played the "Wild West scalping trick a little too brazenly."

The key figure in mobilizing support for the Pueblos was a gaunt, bespectacled, and intensely idealistic social worker named John Collier. An aristocratic Georgian, Collier had learned to respect differing cultures while working with European immigrants in New York City. He became intrigued with the Pueblos in 1920 during a Christmas stopover at Taos. As he watched their Red Deer Dance and other rituals, Collier experienced something of an epiphany. He wrote that he had discovered a "Red Atlantis"—a primitive culture whose sense of community and harmony had been lost by Western man and might provide a model for America's materialistic, industrial society. "They had what the world has lost," he wrote later with characteristic passion for Indians in general. "What the world has lost, the world must have again lest it die. . .the ancient reverence and passion for the earth and the web of life. . . ."

Collier became, in the words of his son, a "lobbyist for the American Indian." He undertook defense of the Pueblos as a research agent for the two-million-member General Federation of Women's Clubs. A keen publicist who wrote magazine articles to further the cause by day and classical verse by night, he orchestrated a diverse range of reform groups. The campaign proved so skillful that the Bursum Bill was defeated and a Collier-backed compromise acceptable to Indians and reformers was approved by Congress. The Pueblo Lands Act of 1924 essentially reversed the provisions of the Bursum Bill by placing the burden of proof of ownership on the non-Indian settlers. It established a special Pueblo Lands Board to determine the extent and status of all Pueblo holdings and provided compensation for any Pueblo land and water rights lost in adjudication of claims.

On another issue affecting the Pueblos, however, the unity shown by reformers crumbled. Collier and his newly created lobbying group, the

Philip Wildshoe, a wealthy Coeur d'Alene farmer, takes his family and friends for a ride in his new 1910 Chalmers convertible. After the Coeur d'Alene abandoned the buffalo in the 1870s, the Idaho-based tribe took up agriculture and became one the most prosperous groups in the Northwest.

American Indian Defense Association, harshly attacked the Indian Bureau's renewed attempts to suppress ceremonial practices, especially the dance rituals of the Pueblos. The bureau had been spurred by complaints from missionaries and from reformers of the Indian Rights Association that the ceremonials consumed too much valuable time and that some permitted "gross sexual immorality."

A series of edicts from the commissioner of Indian affairs sought to ban all manner of ceremonial dances. His objections ranged from snake handling—directed at the Hopi Snake Dance—to "immoral relations between the sexes" to "prolonged periods of celebration which bring the Indians together from remote points to the neglect of their crops, livestock,

and home interest." Collier mounted a campaign based on the constitutionally guaranteed freedom of worship. Although some Christian converts among the Pueblo Indians sided with the commissioner, Collier's campaign profited from the commissioner's own public relations disasters, such as ordering the jailing of nine Pueblo leaders "for violating the bureau's religious crimes code." A congressional measure intended to give the orders the force of law was defeated in 1926, providing Collier and the Pueblos with another victory.

Stressing concepts of cultural pluralism and self-determination that ran against the grain of traditional federal reformers, Collier continued to attack the Bureau of Indian Affairs. He questioned the longstanding practice of using tribal funds that were held in trust by the federal government to finance irrigation projects, roads, and other improvements on Indian land that actually benefited whites more than Indians. He launched a lobbying blitz against a scheme concocted in 1922 by the then secretary of the interior, Albert Fall—subsequently convicted of taking a bribe in the Teapot Dome oil scandal—to exploit oil on certain Indian lands. The plan would have taken away subsurface mineral rights from the Navajo and other tribes who possessed reservations created by presidential

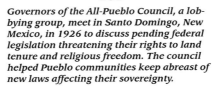

Governors of the All-Pueblo Council, a lobbying group, meet in Santo Domingo, New Mexico, in 1926 to discuss pending federal legislation threatening their rights to land tenure and religious freedom. The council helped Pueblo communities keep abreast of new laws affecting their sovereignty.

John Collier, commissioner of Indian affairs from 1933 to 1945, puts his arms around the shoulders of two Hopi Indians in Oraibi, Arizona. Collier organized the American Indian Defense Association in 1923 and fostered the Indian Reorganization Act of 1934, which revived tribal governments and ended the forced allotment of Indian land.

executive order instead of treaty. The Indian Oil Act of 1927, a direct result of Collier's efforts, repudiated this scheme and awarded all the royalties from oil production on executive-order reservations to the Indians.

T he crescendo of criticism forced the government to reexamine its Indian policies. In 1926 the secretary of the interior commissioned a comprehensive study of Indian affairs by the Institute for Government Research, a privately endowed organization that later merged into the Brookings Institution. The project's staff of 10 specialists in education, health, economics, and other disciplines included Henry Roe Cloud, a Yale-educated Winnebago teacher, Presbyterian minister, former leader in the Society of American Indians, and founder of a prep school for Indian boys. These investigators spent seven months in field research, interviewing Indians and government officials and gathering statistical data.

To the surprise of Collier and other critics who expected a whitewash, the results were devastating to the Indian Bureau. The findings were published in 1928 under the innocuous title *The Problem of Indian Administration,* but quickly became known as the Meriam Report, after the staff director, Lewis Meriam. "An overwhelming majority of Indians are poor," it stated, "even extremely poor." Then, in nearly 850 pages, the report documented in shocking detail the "deplorable conditions" among the nation's Native Americans. It described poor schooling, dire poverty, inadequate housing, malnutrition, and scandalous health care. Boarding schools were overcrowded and "grossly inadequate," and state illiteracy rates were as high as 67 percent. Nearly half of all Indians lived on a per capita income of less than $200 a year, while the U.S. average was nearly $1,350. The Indian Bureau's medical budget allowed about 50 cents a person per year for field treatment, and the statistics reflected this parsimony. The infant mortality rate was double that of the general population, and the death rate from tuberculosis was more than 17 times the national average.

The Meriam Report placed much of the blame for Indian woes on the practice of allotment. This policy, which aimed at assimilation of Indians, had instead demoralized and impoverished them, taking away the resources necessary to facilitate their merger into white society. In their recommendations, the authors flatly called for an end to allotment. They also advocated de-emphasis of distant boarding schools in favor of day schools near home, the formation of Indian cooperatives, and the appropriation of greatly increased funding for health and education. The report even made a bow to the idea of cultural pluralism. While not disavowing assimilation, the authors urged the government to accommodate the person "who wants to remain an Indian and live according to his old culture. . . ." Meriam and his colleagues had set the stage for a new kind of reform, and when radical change started in earnest five years later, the head of the Indian Bureau would be its former harshest critic, John Collier.

When Collier was named commissioner of Indian affairs in 1933 by the new president, Franklin D. Roosevelt, he brought his characteristic energy to the job. His first priority was to provide some measure of economic relief. Reservations already afflicted with poverty were now so desperately in the grip of the Great Depression that emergency shipments of flour and army surplus clothing had to be sent to keep the Indians from starving or freezing to death. To funnel money into the reservations, Collier made certain that Indians shared in the jobs being created by the agencies proliferating under Roosevelt's New Deal and popularly known by their initials: the Civilian Conservation Corps (CCC), Civil Works Administration (CWA), Works Progress Administration (WPA), Public Works Administration (PWA), and National Youth Administration (NYA).

Under the auspices of one or another of these agencies, on or near the reservation, Indians suddenly had paying jobs. They built roads and dams, constructed schools, drilled wells, and planted trees. The WPA hired Indian artists to paint murals on government buildings and to make rugs and pottery for government offices. The Indian Division of the CCC established 72 camps on 33 reservations and paid workers $30 a month primarily for forest and soil restoration projects. More than 85,000 Indians eventually participated in the CCC. At the Rosebud Reservation in South Dakota, about 75 percent of the men worked for the CCC at one time or another, enabling the Lakota to climb—in the words of one Sioux writer—"from absolute deprivation to mere poverty."

At the same time, Collier embarked on a program of radical reform derived from the Meriam Report and from his own lobbying agenda over the past decade. He canceled the outstanding debts against tribal treasuries—ultimately amounting to $12 million—for projects undertaken without Indian approval. He ordered an end to the sale of allotted lands. Most important, he moved decisively to mandate the "fullest constitutional liberty, in all matters affecting religion, conscience, and culture." His policy was clear: "No interference with Indian religious life or ceremonial expression will hereafter be tolerated." In this regard, Collier abolished the requirement that students at government schools attend worship services conducted by the missionaries. In fact, missionaries were being displaced in Washington as well as on the reservation. Where once representatives of the Christian faiths had been invited to advise and assist the commissioner, Collier now called upon social scientists.

Collier also moved to improve the education and health of people on the reservations. He stepped up the bureau's existing policy of shutting down boarding schools in favor of reservation-based day schools that could serve as community centers. Under this program, the number of day schools increased, tripling enrollment there, while the number of boarding school students declined by one-third. In many of these schools, Indians could now learn such new subjects as tribal history—and learn in two languages, English and the student's own native tongue. To bolster medical care, the federal government built new hospitals on the reservations. It also fostered research that found a cure for trachoma, the contagious inflammation of the eye that was one of the great scourges of Indian schools and reservations, leading all too often to blindness. A disease that had affected 30 percent of Indians soon afflicted only five percent.

From Collier's standpoint, the heart of what came to be known as the Indian New Deal was the legislative package submitted to Congress early in 1934. Titled the Indian Reorganization Act (IRA), it contained four main sections that represented a sharp reversal of past policy: Tribes could organize their own governments, which could also act as corporations to borrow federal money and conduct business enterprises; the federal government would promote the study of Indian civilization, including arts, crafts, and traditions, and Indians would be given preference for jobs in the Indian Bureau; the allotment system would be abolished and unsold surplus lands returned to the tribes, which could regain some allotted lands through purchase and the recovery of tracts that would ordinarily pass to the heirs upon the owner's death; and a national Court of Indian Affairs would be established to hear, in the place of federal courts, major criminal cases and controversies affecting the newly organized tribal governments.

Collier's IRA proposal was unprecedented in its appreciation for Indian culture and concern for Indian self-determination, and he took an equally novel step to explain his proposals and gain Indian support. He decided to do what no commissioner had ever done: go to the Indians themselves. He convened a series of 10 Indian congresses at reservations across the United States, from South Dakota to New Mexico to California and Oregon, attended by representatives from practically every tribe. Collier went to many of the congresses himself, coming up against physical

Luther Standing Bear, a Lakota Sioux born in a tipi in 1868 and sent to the Carlisle Indian Industrial School at the age of 10, grew up to become an Indian rights activist. Through his writings, he increased white understanding of traditional Plains culture and raised the public's awareness of the deplorable conditions on many reservations.

exhaustion as well as the Indian's traditional suspicion of the government. At the very first congress in South Dakota, Oliver Prue, a Sioux from the Rosebud Reservation, warned him, "We have come to learn to distrust all government officials that come out here to negotiate with our people." Doing his utmost to dispel this feeling, Collier talked so much that he lost his voice, but he gained an Indian nickname. A Sioux by the name of Sam La Pointe dubbed him "iron man" because "I know he has worn out every interpreter we have got."

Although the majority of the Indians at the meetings favored Collier's bill, many voiced opposition. He had expected dissent from vested interests such as the missionaries because of his advocacy of religious freedom and from old-line reform organizations that feared a retreat from assimilation. But his idealized view of Indians and his work with the Pueblos in New Mexico, with their group orientation, close-knit communities, and limited contact with whites, had not prepared him for the diversity, individualism, and keen sense of human self-interest he encountered in his travels.

Blackfeet tipis rise alongside comfortable tourist lodges at Glacier National Park near Browning, Montana, in the 1920s. The Great Northern Railroad paid the Indians to set up the encampment as a promotional gimmick to attract white vacationers.

Hoping to make a sale at East Glacier Lodge, Medicine Boss Ribs sits by his creations—miniature tipis. Other Blackfeet profited from the tourist trade by performing ceremonial dances, posing for pictures, and selling handicrafts.

Everywhere Collier found dissent. Seltica, a Yakima, said his tribe rejected the IRA because they wanted to continue to live under the provisions of their treaty of 1855. An Oregon man feared true tribal autonomy might make his people "feel like a child who would get lost when his guide left him." In Oklahoma, James Otipoby asserted that Comanches "love our allotments and don't want to be segregated." Other Oklahoma Indians worried about losing their oil and mineral rights.

George White Bull, a Standing Rock Sioux, also feared that the bill would jeopardize ownership of personal allotments. Such expressions of individualism stunned Collier. He was amazed by the extent to which Indians had accepted the American way of ownership and rejected the

No. 1874

The United States of America,

To all to whom these presents shall come, GREETING.

Whereas, There has been deposited in the General Land Office of the United States a schedule of allotments of land, dated May 23, 1901 from the Commissioner of Indian Affairs, approved by the Secretary of the Interior, May 23, 1901 whereby it appears that under the provisions of the sixth section of the Act of Congress approved June 6, 1900 (31 Stats., 672) James Laptto a Kiowa Indian residing on the Kiowa, Comanche, and Apache Reservation has been allotted the following-described land, viz:

The South East quarter of Section twenty in Township five North of Range eighteen West of the Indian Meridian in Oklahoma, containing one hundred and sixty acres,

Now know ye, That the United States of America, in consideration of the premises and in accordance with the provisions of the fifth section of the Act of Congress of February 8, 1887 (24 Stats., 388), **HEREBY DECLARES** that it does and will hold the land thus allotted, subject to all the restrictions and conditions contained in said fifth section as modified by the fifth article of the agreement ratified by said sixth section of the Act of June 6, 1900, for the period of twenty-five years, in trust for the sole use and benefit of the said James Laptto or or in case of his decease, for the sole use of his heirs, according to the laws of the State or Territory where such land is located, and that at the expiration of said period the United States will convey the same by patent to said Indian, or his heirs, as aforesaid, in fee, discharged of said trust and free of all charge or incumbrance whatsoever.

In testimony whereof, I, William McKinley President of the United States of America, have caused these Letters to be made Patent and the Seal of the General Land Office to be hereunto affixed.

Given under my hand at the City of Washington, this twenty-fifth day of August , in the year of our Lord one thousand nine hundred and one and of the Independence of the United States, the one hundred and twenty-sixth

By the President: William McKinley

By J. M. McKean , Secretary.

C. M. Bush

Recorder of the General Land Office.

Recorded Vol. 84 p. 365

A certificate of allotment, dated May 23, 1901, grants a Kiowa named James Laptto 160 acres of land. Imprinted on the General Land Office seal are an American eagle and a plow.

Flathead Reservation delegates Victor Vandenberg and Martin Charlo present a ceremonial club to Harold Ickes, the U.S. secretary of the interior, in 1935. Ickes had just given them a constitution establishing a tribal government for the confederated Kootenai and Salish tribes.

communal control that once had characterized many of the tribes. "I am 100 percent American," said a California woman. "I tell you this bill preaches communism and socialism."

Surprised but undaunted, Collier and his associates drafted more than 30 amendments to deal with objections. They especially tried to address the concerns about loss of personal allotments, eliminating the provision that prevented inheritance of allotments and protecting individual ownership of mineral rights. None of this was enough for Congress, which fashioned its own version of the Indian Reorganization Act of 1934. The final act stripped away some of Collier's most controversial proposals, such as the Court of Indian Affairs, and watered down the statement of support for preserving Indian culture. Congress also placed tight restrictions on the mechanisms for transfer of previously allotted land to tribal jurisdiction, making it voluntary rather than mandatory. Oklahoma and the Alaska Territory were excluded from most of the sections of the act, but two years later, they were brought under more of its provisions by special legislation.

Whatever Collier's disappointment at failure to get the whole loaf, it was a stunning achievement nonetheless. The most extraordinary triumph was putting an end to all future allotments. Launched in 1887 as a means of breaking up tribes and assimilating their members, the federal allotment policy had succeeded mainly in rendering "whole tribes totally landless," Collier wrote. During the 47 years since passage of the Dawes Act, allotment had shrunk the Indian land base by almost two-thirds—from 138 million acres to 48 million acres. Nearly half of the loss had been land declared surplus by the government and sold; two-thirds of the rest was accounted for by allotments sold to non-Indians. Much of the land that remained in Indian hands consisted of holdings on reservations that were probably never allotted because they were valueless—arid or otherwise unsuitable—and whites did not covet them. Belatedly, allotment had now ended, although the goal of assimilation that drove it had not disappeared but only changed in its means and time schedule. Tribal community, once seen as the obstacle to immediate assimilation, now became the hoped-for means of achieving integration into the larger society in the long run.

Enactment of the bill was only the beginning. One of the provisions inserted by Congress allowed each tribe to decide for itself whether the act would apply to its people. These referendums brought further campaigning for and against the IRA. Collier complained that, in a "deliberate campaign to mislead the Indians," opponents were stressing controversial aspects of the original bill that had been eliminated in the final version. According to a ruling by government lawyers, a tribe could not be excluded from the act unless a majority of all eligible voters cast ballots against the bill. Those who boycotted the election, however, were counted as voting for the IRA. After this ruling proved decisive in reversing an otherwise negative vote in 17 small tribes, Congress passed special legislation: Henceforth, a majority of those actually voting, when at least 30 percent of the population turned out, and not those merely eligible, would determine acceptance or rejection.

More than two-thirds of the tribes voted in favor of coverage by the IRA. Votes of approval came from 181 tribes with a total of 129,750 members; rejections came from 77 tribes with 86,365 members. (Fourteen other groups did not hold elections and thus automatically came under the act.) As expected, the six-nation Iroquois of New York went overwhelmingly against the bill. The Crow and the Klamath surprisingly voted against participation, but Collier's greatest disappointment came from the most populous tribe of all, the Navajo.

Collier had harbored high hopes for the Navajo. Their vast reservation, spread over four states, had not been touched by allotment, and traditional institutions remained largely intact. But the 40,000-member tribe had been thrown into turmoil by a previous and controversial government program to remedy overgrazing and soil erosion on Navajo rangelands by reducing the herds of sheep, goats, and horses. After voluntary measures failed, Collier ordered the destruction of tens of thousands of sheep. Livestock was a way of life for many Navajos, a measure of social status as well as source of livelihood. Owners of small sheep herds who depended on the wool for subsistence were particularly hard hit. "You have cut off my arms," a Navajo herdsman told government officials after they took some of his sheep. "You have cut off my legs. You have taken my head off. There is nothing left for me." When the man fell ill and died a few months later, his wife blamed it all on the loss of their sheep.

The leader of Navajo opposition to Collier's policies, Jacob C. Morgan, took full advantage of such grief. A graduate of Hampton Institute, Morgan had returned to the reservation early in the 20th century determined to help his tribesmen integrate into the American mainstream. Convinced that Collier's policies represented a step backward for his people, Morgan campaigned vigorously against the IRA, skillfully linking it to the livestock reduction plan in the minds of voters. Nearly 98 percent of the eligible Navajos took part in the 1935 referendum, rejecting the IRA by 419 votes. Bitter at the defeat, Collier reminded the Navajo that they had deprived themselves of $1 million dollars in IRA grants and loans for the following year.

Those groups that voted to come under the act faced the task of adopting a constitution and organizing their own governments. Most were ill prepared to deal with the white man's way of achieving this. One problem was that they were being asked to form tribal governments when tradition called for organization on the basis of smaller-scale bands or villages. Another difficulty was the general unfamiliarity with Anglo-Saxon concepts such as majority rule, which contrasted with the practice in many groups of involving all members and reaching a consensus before taking action. Local cultural attitudes sometimes made the process more difficult. Many Hopis voted against their proposed constitution because they feared it would subject elected council delegates to public criticism— a dreadful sanction in their culture. Other Hopis rejected the constitution because the mark of an X required to cast a favorable vote resembled the cross that symbolized the hated Spaniards who once had ruled them.

The process of instituting self-government also frequently stirred divisiveness rather than the solidarity Collier sought. The factionalism on the South Dakota Sioux reservations typified the political discord. A group of young educated Indians, usually of mixed blood, who enthusiastically embraced the IRA brand of tribal councils were known as the New Dealers. They were pitted against older traditionalists, or Old Dealers, often full blooded. In an earlier time, it would have been the custom for the dissenters to pull up stakes and move to another patch of the Plains, but now there was no place to go, so they had to stay and continue the debate. Given such difficulties, only about half the groups who accepted the IRA actually drafted constitutions and established tribal governments.

The powers of the new tribal councils were limited to a kind of home rule. Like a municipality, the council could conduct elections, create courts, and perform other local functions. The fact that the secretary of the interior could veto their decisions prompted some Indians to suggest that the whole business was a sham. "It's not self-government," asserted Ramon Roubideaux, a Sioux attorney, "because self-government by permission is no self-government at all."

Members of the Blackfeet tribal council gather to dedicate an oil well on their Montana reservation in 1928. The council encouraged the leasing of reservation land for oil as a means of providing employment for their fellow tribesmen.

Comanche chief and peyote roadman Quanah Parker (far left) stands in a wagon with other tribal leaders. Their traditional braids combined with cowboy hats, shirts, vests, and trousers attest to the changing patterns of Indian dress during the late 19th and early 20th centuries.

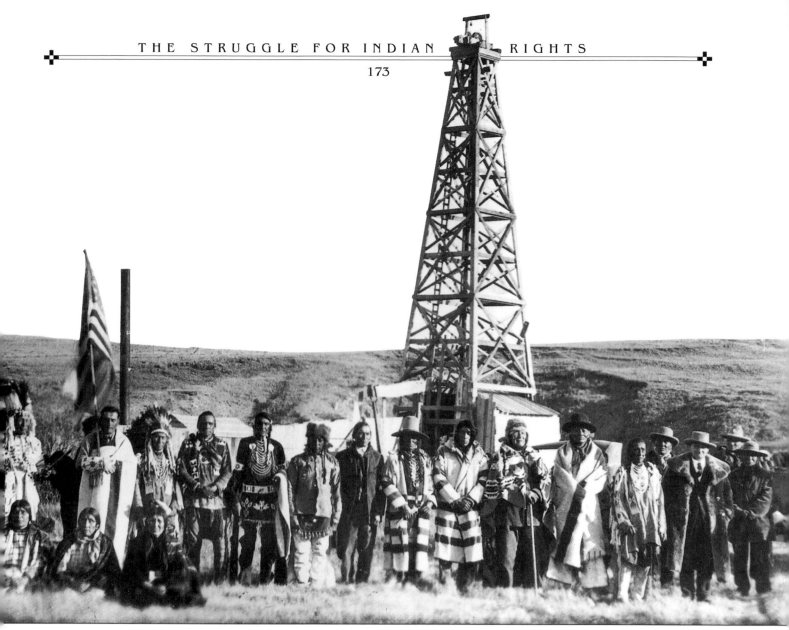

The economic gains under the IRA proved to be less than hoped for but helpful nonetheless. With federal aid, tribal councils were able to re-acquire over a 13-year period a modest amount of land previously lost in the allotment process—nearly four million acres. Loans from the IRA's $5 million revolving credit fund financed projects in 82 tribes. Although many of the loans were funneled to individual entrepreneurs to buy seed, im-prove their livestock herds, or purchase commercial fishing boats, tribal governments also undertook the kind of communal enterprises close to Collier's heart. The Northern Cheyenne of Montana borrowed funds to de-velop their cattle herds. The Ojibwa of Wisconsin constructed cabins to attract tourists. The Mescalero Apache of New Mexico, who had adopted a constitution after staging a series of popular plays to illustrate its benefits, built housing to replace a camp of brush tipis and board shacks, increased farm production eightfold, and expanded their cooperative cattle industry.

Other programs of the Indian New Deal helped ease poverty on the reservation. Creation of the Indian Arts and Crafts Board gave national recognition to their artistic heritage and promoted the making and marketing of products ranging from Alaskan woodcarvings to Navajo jewelry and Pueblo pottery. The number of Native Americans employed by the Indian Bureau increased more than 20-fold. And an estimated $100 million from other New Deal relief and recovery agencies poured into the reservations.

Many years later, the author Vine Deloria Jr., a member of the Standing Rock Sioux, fondly recalled visiting a project of special resonance as a young boy: "In the canyons north of Allen, South Dakota, a beautiful buffalo pasture was built by the CCC, and the whole area was transformed into a recreation wonderland. Indians would come from miles around to see the buffalo and leave with a strange look in their eyes. Many times I stood silently watching while old men talked to the buffalo about the old days. They would conclude by singing a song before respectfully departing, their eyes filled with tears and their minds occupied with the memories of other times and places. It was difficult to determine who was the captive—the buffalo fenced in or the Indian fenced out."

Collier wanted to do more, but Congress grew increasingly reluctant to pay for the Indian New Deal. One measure of this unwillingness was the refusal to appropriate more than half of the $10 million promised for the IRA revolving credit fund. Congress demonstrated growing acrimony as well as parsimony. Committees in both houses provided a forum for Collier's most fervent critic, the American Indian Federation. Small but vociferous, the federation was led by Joseph Bruner, a Creek businessman and a disciple of Carlos Montezuma, the late Yavapai-Apache physician who had wanted to liberate Indians from all federal controls. The rhetoric frequently turned ugly. Alice Lee Jemison, a Seneca from New York and a federation member, kept up a drumbeat of criticism, urging repeal of the IRA and calling for the dismissal of John Collier on the grounds that he was a Communist and an atheist. Collier fought back, dismissing her charges as "glimmerings on the lunatic fringe."

Collier and his supporters managed to stave off attempts in Congress to repeal or cripple the IRA, but the United States' entry into World War II effectively stalled the Indian New Deal. Collier would end his 12 years in office in 1945—the longest tenure of any commissioner. Life on the reservation remained grim, but much had changed. Forces had been set in motion that would inspire future Indian activists. Henry Roe Cloud, the Winnebago who helped found the Society of American Indians, praised Collier for his work, declaring that he had spurred a rebirth of pride. Indians could now feel, he wrote, that they possessed a "great history, and great thoughts, and great ideas and inspirations in our hearts." ❖

Brandishing wrenches, Winnebago, Sioux, and Pawnee army air corps recruits attending mechanic's school at Sheppard Field, Texas, good-naturedly perform an improvised dance for their fellow trainees during World War II. Between 1942 and 1945, more than 25,000 Indians served in both the Pacific and the European theaters, and at least 40,000 others left the reservations each year to work in war industries.

MENDING THE BROKEN HOOP

On December 23, 1890, Chief Big Foot, or Si Tanka, led his band of 350 Miniconjou Sioux away from their Cheyenne River Reservation in South Dakota. Big Foot knew that the army planned to arrest him as a leader of the Ghost Dance movement, which promised to restore Lakotas to freedom and power, and he feared that his people would be punished as well.

Braving bitter cold, the Miniconjous headed south through the Badlands toward the Pine Ridge Agency, where they hoped to find refuge with other Lakotas. On December 28, however, the Indians were intercepted by cavalry and escorted to Wounded Knee Creek. There they were surrounded by nearly 500 soldiers, who moved to disarm the Lakotas the next morning. A scuffle ensued, and shooting broke out. Soon troops were firing indiscriminately on men, women, and children as they attempted to escape. More than 200 Lakotas died, including Big Foot himself.

After the massacre, declared the Oglala holy man Black Elk, his people were no longer one circle. "The nation's hoop is broken and scattered," he lamented.

Nearly a century later, in 1986, a group of Lakotas known as the Big Foot Memorial Riders set out to mend that hoop. Beginning on December 23, they retraced Big Foot's path to Wounded Knee. They repeated the journey during the following years, and in 1990, the 100th anniversary of the massacre, they rode off one last time *(right)*. "Once this ceremony is done, we look to the future," said Birgil Kills Straight, the main organizer of the event. With mourning behind them, he added, Lakotas would enter "a new world, a new beginning."

ig Foot and his band of Lakotas traveled the 150-mile route shown at left through the Badlands in 1890 before they were surrounded and massacred at Wounded Knee Creek. One hundred years later, the Big Foot Memorial Riders followed the same route to pay tribute to the victims and "wipe away the tears" of their descendants.

*L*akotas carrying ceremonial staffs lead
the way as the memorial riders leave the
town of Bridger on the Cheyenne River Reservation early on December 23, 1990, the first

*R*iders cross the frozen Cheyenne River on the opening leg of their journey, conducted in temperatures approaching 30 degrees below zero. Spread out in single file to avoid breaking through weak spots in the ice, the riders continued on to their first camp, situated on a farm about 30 miles to the south. Riders considered themselves fortunate compared with Big Foot and his people, most of whom covered this stretch of the trip on foot in similar weather. "They wore moccasins and castoff clothing," one Lakota observed. "They didn't have insulated boots and rubber overshoes."

*R*iders gather in a prayer circle at Red Water Creek Camp, which they reached on the third day after crossing perilous Big Foot Pass in the Badlands (below), where Si Tanka and his followers had barely eluded cavalry patrols in 1890. The memorial riders said special prayers each day for children and the elderly, for the sick and for those in prison, for women and Mother Earth—and for the survival of their culture and traditions.

The riders remained in camp here at Red Water Creek on the fourth day, resting as Big Foot did during his journey. The chief had contracted pneumonia and traveled most of the way to Wounded Knee in the back of a wagon, wrapped in blankets and coughing up blood. During the respite here, many memorial riders took time to visit family and friends on the Pine Ridge Reservation, home of the Oglala Sioux, whom Big Foot's people had looked to for support.

On the sixth day, December 28, more than 300 riders descend Porcupine Butte amid blowing snow to the spot where Big Foot's hungry and weary band was intercepted by troops and conducted to Wounded Knee. Sub-zero temperatures and sharp winds made this the cruelest day yet for the riders. The horses were slowed by the snow and ice that became encrusted on their hoofs and legs (above). The riders related that they found the strength to carry on by praying to the ancestors who had suffered here before them.

On December 29, 1990, 100 years to the day after the massacre, riders pass through purifying sage smoke (below) as they enter the cemetery at Wounded Knee to conduct a Wiping of Tears Ceremony at the mass grave of Si Tanka and his slain followers. The ceremony marked the end of mourning for the victims, in keeping with a Lakota prophecy declaring that seven generations of sorrow would lead to a resurgence of hope for the Lakota Nation.

A large monument, erected by Lakotas in 1903, marks the enclosed resting place of 146 men, women, and children found dead at the massacre site. Many others died later from wounds or from exposure after fleeing from the soldiers. Following the ceremony in 1990, organizer Alex White Plume spoke of a brighter future: "The unity of the people will mend the hoop."

Two onlookers wrapped in a colorful Lakota quilt pay their respects as riders form a circle around the mass grave for the Wiping of Tears. During the ceremony, Arvol Looking Horse, keeper of the sacred pipe of the Lakota, offered a prayer of peace for all descendants of those who died at Wounded Knee and asked that the United States revoke the Congressional Medals of Honor awarded to a number of the soldiers who took part in the attack.

A woman cries while leaving flowers at the grave site of a loved one. Grief for the victims of Wounded Knee and other departed friends and kin ran deep during the ceremony, even as people tried to put sorrow behind them. As one rider said afterward, "The Lakota Nation's greatest tragedy was used to build the people's strength."

ACKNOWLEDGMENTS

The editors wish to thank the following individuals and institutions for their valuable assistance in the preparation of this volume:

In the United States:

Arizona: Phoenix—Richard Pearce-Moses, The Heard Museum.
Colorado: Boulder—Diana Leonard, University of Colorado Museum.
Nebraska: Lincoln—John Carter, Marty Miller, Nebraska State Historical Society.
Nevada: Las Vegas—Dr. Willard Rollings, University of Nevada.
New Mexico: Fairacres—Oscar Branson. Santa Fe—Arthur Olivas, Willow Powers, Museum of New Mexico.
Texas: San Antonio—Jack Judson.
Washington, D.C.: Vyrtis Thomas, National Anthropological Archives, Smithsonian Institution.

BIBLIOGRAPHY

BOOKS

All Roads Are Good. Washington, D.C.: Smithsonian Institution Press, 1994.

America's Fascinating Indian Heritage. Pleasantville, N.Y.: Reader's Digest Association, 1978.

Apess, William. *On Our Own Ground.* Ed. by Barry O'Connell. Amherst: University of Massachusetts Press, 1992.

Axtell, James. *The Invasion Within.* New York: Oxford University Press, 1985.

Bass, Althea. *The Arapaho Way.* New York: Clarkson N. Potter, 1966.

Bennitt, Mark, comp. *History of the Louisiana Purchase Exposition.* St. Louis: Universal Exposition Publishing, 1905.

Bernotas, Bob. *Sitting Bull: Chief of the Sioux.* New York: Chelsea House Publishers, 1992.

Berthrong, Donald J. *The Southern Cheyennes.* Norman: University of Oklahoma Press, 1963.

Biolsi, Thomas. *Organizing the Lakota.* Tucson: University of Arizona Press, 1992.

Blanchard, David S. *Kahnawake.* Kahnawake, Que.: Kanien'kehaka Raotitiohkwa Press, 1980.

Bonnin, Gertrude, Charles H. Fabens, and Matthew K. Sniffen. *Oklahoma's Poor Rich Indians.* Philadelphia: Office of the Indian Rights Association, 1924.

Burns, Louis F. *A History of the Osage People.* Fallbrook, Calif.: Ciga Press, 1989.

Bush, Alfred L. *The Photograph and the American Indian.* Princeton, N.J.: Princeton University Press, 1994.

Calloway, Colin G., ed. *The World Turned Upside Down.* Boston: Bedford Books of St. Martin's Press, 1994.

Calloway, Colin G., ed. and comp. *Dawnland Encounters.* Hanover, N.H.: University Press of New England, 1991.

Campisi, Jack. *The Mashpee Indians.* Syracuse, N.Y.: Syracuse University Press, 1991.

Champagne, Duane. *Native America.* Detroit: Visible Ink Press, 1994.

Charging Eagle, Tom, and Ron Zeilinger. *Black Hills: Sacred Hills.* Chamberlain, S.Dak.: Tipi Press, 1987.

Coleman, Michael C. *American Indian Children at School, 1850-1930.* Jackson: University Press of Mississippi, 1993.

Coolidge, Dane, and Mary Roberts Coolidge. *The Navajo Indians.* Boston: Houghton Mifflin, 1930.

Davis, Leslie B., ed. *Lifeways of Intermontane and Plains Montana Indians.* Bozeman: Montana State University, 1979.

Deloria, Vine, Jr. *Behind the Trail of Broken Treaties.* New York: Delacorte Press, 1974.

Deloria, Vine, Jr., ed. *American Indian Policy in the Twentieth Century.* Norman: University of Oklahoma Press, 1985.

Deloria, Vine, Jr., and Clifford M. Lytle. *The Nations Within.* New York: Pantheon Books, 1984.

Demos, John. *The Unredeemed Captive.* New York: Alfred A. Knopf, 1994.

Dickason, Olive Patricia. *Canada's First Nations.* Norman: University of Oklahoma Press, 1992.

Dillon, Richard H. *North American Indian Wars.* New York: Gallery Books, 1983.

Ewers, John C., Helen M. Mangelsdorf, and William S. Wierzbowski. *Images of a Vanished Life.* Philadelphia: Pennsylvania Academy of the Fine Arts, 1985.

Farr, William E. *The Reservation Blackfeet, 1882-1945.* Seattle: University of Washington Press, 1984.

Ferris, Jeri. *Native American Doctor: The Story of Susan LaFlesche Picotte.* Minneapolis: Carolrhoda Books, 1991.

Fire, John/Lame Deer, and Richard Erdoes. *Lame Deer: Seeker of Visions.* New York: Simon and Schuster, 1972.

The Forest City: Comprising the Official Photographic Views of the Universal Exposition Held in Saint Louis, 1904. St. Louis: N. D. Thompson Publishing, 1904.

Freedman, Russell. *Indian Chiefs.* New York: Holiday House, 1987.

Garbarino, Merwyn S. *Native American Heritage.* Prospect Heights, Ill.: Waveland Press, 1985.

Geronimo. *Geronimo's Story of His Life.* Ed. by S. M. Barrett. New York: Duffield & Co., 1906.

Gibson, Arrell Morgan:
 The American Indian. Lexington, Mass.: D. C. Heath, 1980.
 The Kickapoos. Norman: University of Oklahoma Press, 1963.

Gilman, Carolyn, and Mary Jane Schneider. *The Way to Independence.* St. Paul: Minnesota Historical Society Press, 1987.

Green, L. C., and Olive P. Dickason. *The Law of Nations and the New World.* Edmonton: University of Alberta Press, 1989.

Griffen, William B. *Apaches at War and Peace: The Janos Presidio, 1750-1858.* Albuquerque: University of New Mexico, 1988.

Hagan, William T.:
 American Indians. Chicago: University of Chicago Press, 1961.
 Indian Police and Judges. New Haven, Conn.: Yale University Press, 1966.
 Quanah Parker, Comanche Chief. Norman: University of Oklahoma Press, 1993.

The Sac and Fox Indians. Norman: University of Oklahoma Press, 1958.

Hall, Thomas D. *Social Change in the Southwest, 1350-1880.* Lawrence: University Press of Kansas, 1989.

Hauptman, Laurence M. *The Iroquois and the New Deal.* Syracuse, N.Y.: Syracuse University Press, 1981.

Hirschfelder, Arlene, and Paulette Molin. *The Encyclopedia of Native American Religions.* New York: Facts On File, 1992.

Hopkins, Sarah Winnemucca. *Life among the Paiutes.* Ed. by Mrs. Horace Mann. Bishop, Calif.: Sierra Media, 1969.

Hoxie, Frederick E. *A Final Promise.* Lincoln: University of Nebraska Press, 1984.

Hoxie, Frederick E., ed. *Indians in American History.* Arlington Heights, Ill.: Harlan Davidson, 1988.

Hultgren, Mary Lou, and Paulette Fairbanks Molin. *To Lead and To Serve.* Charlottesville: Virginia Foundation for the Humanities and Public Policy, 1989.

Irredeemable America. Ed. by Imre Sutton. Albuquerque: University of New Mexico, 1985.

Iverson, Peter. *When Indians Became Cowboys.* Norman: University of Oklahoma Press, 1994.

Iverson, Peter, ed. *The Plains Indians of the Twentieth Century.* Norman: University of Oklahoma Press, 1985.

Jackson, Curtis E., and Marcia J. Galli. *A History of the Bureau of Indian Affairs and Its Activities among Indians.* San Francisco: R & E Research Associates, 1977.

Jennings, Francis. *The Invasion of America.* Chapel Hill: University of North Carolina Press, 1975.

Josephy, Alvin M., Jr.:
 500 Nations. New York: Alfred A. Knopf, 1994.
 Now That the Buffalo's Gone. New York: Alfred A. Knopf, 1985.

Josephy, Alvin M., Jr., Trudy Thomas, and Jeanne Eder. *Wounded Knee: Lest We Forget.* Cody, Wyo.: Buffalo Bill Historical Center, 1990.

Kehoe, Alice Beck. *The Ghost Dance.* New York: Holt, Rinehart and Winston, 1989.

Kelly, Lawrence C.:
 The Assault on Assimilation. Albuquerque: University of New Mexico Press, 1983.
 Federal Indian Policy. New York: Chelsea House Publishers, 1990.

Kersey, Harry A., Jr. *The Florida Seminoles and the New Deal: 1933-1942.* Boca Raton: Florida Atlantic University Press, 1989.

Lazarus, Edward. *Black Hills, White Justice.* New York: Harper Collins, 1991.

Leacock, Eleanor Burke, and Nancy Oestreich Lurie, eds. *North American Indians in Historical*

Perspective. New York: Random House, 1971.

Lomawaima, K. Tsianina. *They Called It Prairie Light: The Story of Chilocco Indian School.* Lincoln: University of Nebraska Press, 1994.

Manuel, George, and Michael Posluns. *The Fourth World.* New York: Free Press, 1974.

Manypenny, George W. *Our Indian Wards.* New York: Da Capo Press, 1972.

Matthiessen, Peter. *In the Spirit of Crazy Horse.* New York: Viking Press, 1983.

McAuliffe, Dennis, Jr. *The Deaths of Sybil Bolton.* New York: Times Books, 1994.

McClintock, Walter. *The Old North Trail.* Lincoln: University of Nebraska Press, 1968.

McLuhan, T. C. *Dream Tracks.* New York: Harry N. Abrams, 1985.

Meyer, Melissa L. *The White Earth Tragedy.* Lincoln: University of Nebraska Press, 1994.

Mihesuah, Devon A. *Cultivating the Rosebuds.* Urbana: University of Illinois Press, 1993.

Morton, Richard L. *Colonial Virginia, Volume 1: The Tidewater Period, 1607-1710.* Chapel Hill: University of North Carolina Press, 1960.

Mourning Dove. *Mourning Dove.* Ed. by Jay Miller. Lincoln: University of Nebraska Press, 1990.

Nabokov, Peter, ed. *Native American Testimony.* New York: Penguin Books, 1991.

Paredes, J. Anthony, ed. *Indians of the Southeastern United States in the Late 20th Century.* Tuscaloosa: University of Alabama Press, 1992.

Parker, Dorothy R. *Singing an Indian Song: A Biography of D'Arcy McNickle..* Lincoln: University of Nebraska Press, 1992.

Parman, Donald L. *The Navajos and the New Deal.* New Haven, Conn.: Yale University Press, 1976.

Peterson, Jacqueline. *Sacred Encounters.* Norman: University of Oklahoma Press, 1993.

Peyer, Bernd, ed. *The Elders Wrote.* Berlin: Dietrich Reimer Verlag, 1982.

Philp, Kenneth R. *John Collier's Crusade for Indian Reform: 1920-1954.* Tucson: University of Arizona Press, 1977.

Porter, Frank W., III. *The Bureau of Indian Affairs.* New York: Chelsea House Publishers, 1988.

The Problem of Indian Administration. Baltimore: Johns Hopkins Press, 1928.

Prucha, Francis Paul:
  American Indian Policy in Crisis. Norman: University of Oklahoma Press, 1976.
  American Indian Policy in the Formative Years. Cambridge, Mass.: Harvard University Press, 1962.
  The Great Father. Vols. 1 and 2. Lincoln: University of Nebraska Press, 1984.

Prucha, Francis Paul, ed. *Documents of United States Indian Policy.* Lincoln: University of Nebraska Press, 1975.

Prucha, Francis Paul, William T. Hagan, and Alvin M. Josephy, Jr. *Indiana Historical Society Lectures, 1970-1971: American Indian Policy.* Indianapolis: Indiana Historical Society, 1971.

Rezatto, Helen. *Tales of the Black Hills.* Rapid City, S.Dak.: Fenwyn Press, 1989.

Richter, Daniel K. *The Ordeal of the Longhouse.* Chapel Hill: University of North Carolina Press, 1992.

Robotham, Tom. *Native Americans in Early Photographs.* San Diego: Thunder Bay Press, 1994.

Rosa, Joseph G., and Robin May. *Buffalo Bill and His Wild West.* Lawrence: University Press of Kansas, 1989.

Rountree, Helen C. *Pocahontas's People.* Norman: University of Oklahoma Press, 1990.

Russell, George. *American Indian Digest.* Phoenix: Thunderbird Enterprises, 1994.

Schmeckebier, Laurence F. *The Office of Indian Affairs.* Baltimore: Johns Hopkins Press, 1927.

Sekaquaptewa, Helen. *Me and Mine.* Comp. by Louise Udall. Tucson: University of Arizona Press, 1969.

Shanks, Ralph. *The North American Indian Travel Guide.* Ed. by Lisa Woo Shanks. Petaluma, Calif.: Costaño Books, 1991.

Sheehan, Bernard W. *Seeds of Extinction.* Chapel Hill: University of North Carolina Press, 1973.

Smith, Rex Alan. *Moon of Popping Trees.* New York: Reader's Digest Press, 1975.

Spicer, Edward H. *Cycles of Conquest.* Tucson: University of Arizona Press, 1962.

Standing Bear, Luther. *My People the Sioux.* Ed. by E. A. Brininstool. Lincoln: University of Nebraska Press, 1975.

Stands In Timber, John, and Margot Liberty. *Cheyenne Memories.* Lincoln: University of Nebraska Press, 1967.

Steiner, Stan. *The New Indians.* New York: Harper & Row, 1968.

Stepney, Philip H. R., and David J. Goa, eds. *The Scriver Blackfoot Collection.* Edmonton: Provincial Museum of Alberta, 1990.

Strickland, Rennard. *The Indians in Oklahoma.* Norman: University of Oklahoma Press, 1980.

Taylor, Theodore W. *The Bureau of Indian Affairs.* Boulder, Colo.: Westview Press, 1984.

Thomas, David Hurst. *The Southwestern Indian Detours.* Phoenix: Hunter Publishing, 1978.

Thomas, David Hurst, et al. *The Native Americans.* Ed. by Betty Ballantine and Ian Ballantine. Atlanta: Turner Publishing, 1993.

Thornton, Russell. *American Indian Holocaust and Survival.* Norman: University of Oklahoma Press, 1987.

Trenholm, Virginia Cole. *The Arapahoes, Our People.* Norman: University of Oklahoma Press, 1970.

Trennert, Robert A., Jr. *Alternative to Extinction.* Philadelphia: Temple University Press, 1975.

Trigger, Bruce G., ed. *Northeast.* Vol. 15 of *Handbook of North American Indians.* Washington, D.C.: Smithsonian Institution, 1978.

Viola, Herman J. *After Columbus.* Washington, D.C.: Smithsonian Institution Press, 1990.

Waldman, Carl. *Encyclopedia of Native American Tribes.* New York: Facts On File, 1988.

Walens, Stanley. *The Kwakiutl.* New York: Chelsea House Publishers, 1992.

Wallace, Anthony F. C.:
  The Death and Rebirth of the Seneca. New York: Vintage Books, 1969.
  The Long, Bitter Trail. New York: Hill and Wang, 1993.

Washburn, Wilcomb E.:
  The Governor and the Rebel. Chapel Hill: University of North Carolina Press, 1957.
  The Indian in America. New York: Harper & Row, 1975.

Washburn, Wilcomb E., ed. *History of Indian-White Relations.* Vol. 4 of *Handbook of North American Indians.* Washington, D.C.: Smithsonian Institution, 1988.

Weber, David J. *The Spanish Frontier in North America.* New Haven, Conn.: Yale University Press, 1992.

White, Richard. *"It's Your Misfortune and None of My Own."* Norman: University of Oklahoma Press, 1991.

The Wild West, by the editors of Time-Life Books. Alexandria, Va.: Time-Life Books, 1993.

Wissler, Clark. *Red Man Reservations.* New York: Collier Books, 1971.

Wood, Ted. *A Boy Becomes a Man at Wounded Knee.* New York: Walker, 1992.

PERIODICALS

Adams, David Wallace. "Education in Hues: Red and Black at Hampton Institute, 1878-1893." *The South Atlantic Quarterly,* Spring 1977.

Ahern, Wilbert H. "The Returned Indians: Hampton Institute and Its Indian Alumni, 1879-1893." *The Journal of Ethnic Studies,* Winter 1983.

Cudmore, Patrick. "The Great American Holocaust." *Lakota Times,* January 8, 1991.

Foster, J. Todd. "Picture No Joke to Family: Magazine Caption Insulting to Tribe." *Spokesman Review,* April 27, 1993.

Fredrickson, Vera Mae, ed. "School Days in Northern California: The Accounts of Six Pomo Women." *News from Native California,* Fall 1989.

Hamley, Jeffrey. "An Introduction to the Federal Indian Boarding School Movement." *North Dakota History: Journal of the Northern Plains,* Spring 1994.

Hultgren, Mary Lou. "American Indian Collections of the Hampton University Museum." *American Indian Art,* Winter 1987.

Little Eagle, Avis. "Mending the Sacred Hoop." *Lakota Times,* January 8, 1991.

Ludlow, Helen W. "Indian Education at Hampton and Carlisle." *Harper's Magazine,* April 1881.

Salisbury, Neal. "Red Puritans: The 'Praying Indians' of Massachusetts Bay and John Eliot." *The William and Mary Quarterly,* 1974, Vol. 31.

Simon, David J. "Healing the Sacred Hoop." *National Parks,* September-October 1991.

Thomas, Peter A. "Contrastive Subsistence Strategies and Land Use As Factors For Understanding Indian-White Relations in New England." *Ethnohistory,* Winter 1976.

OTHER SOURCES

"Buffalo Bill's Wild West." Souvenir program. Cody, Wyo.: Buffalo Bill Historical Center, 1885 reproduction.

Hoxie, Frederick E. "Treaties: A Source Book." Occasional papers in curriculum, #12. Chicago: D'Arcy McNickle Center for the History of the American Indian at the Newberry Library, 1992.

Joint Special Committee, U.S. Congress. "Condition of the Indian Tribes." Report. Washington, D.C.: U.S. Government Printing Office, 1867.

"The Last Years of Sitting Bull." Museum booklet. Bismarck: North Dakota Heritage Center, 1984.

O'Brien, Jean. "Dispossession by Degrees: Indian Land and Identity in Natick, Massachusetts, 1650-1790." Unpublished manuscript.

PICTURE CREDITS

Credits from left to right are separated by semicolons, from top to bottom by dashes.

Cover: © Nebraska State Hist. Soc. **6:** Princeton Collections of Western Americana, Visual Materials Division, Dept. of Rare Books and Special Collections, Princeton Univ. Libraries, photographer: John N. Choate. **7:** Frame courtesy Anne-Louise Gates. Photo courtesy Princeton Collections of Western Americana, Visual Materials Division, Dept. of Rare Books and Special Collections, Princeton Univ. Libraries, photographer: John N. Choate. **8:** Cumberland County Hist. Soc., Carlisle, Pa. **9:** Frame courtesy Anne-Louise Gates. Photo courtesy Cumberland County Hist. Soc., Carlisle, Pa. **10:** © Collection of Lori and Victor Germack. **11:** Frame courtesy Anne-Louise Gates. Photo courtesy © Collection of Lori and Victor Germack. **12:** Hampton Univ. Archives, Hampton, Va. **13:** Frame courtesy Anne-Louise Gates. Photo courtesy Hampton Univ. Archives, Hampton, Va. **14:** Canadian Museum of Civilization, Hull, Que., nos. 590-2304—80-6675. **16, 17:** From *American Indian Holocaust and Survival*, by Russell Thornton. © 1987 by the Univ. of Oklahoma Press. **19:** The American Indian Digest/Thunderbird Enterprises/George Russell. **20:** Bowdoin College Museum of Art, Brunswick, Me., bequest of the Honorable James Bowdoin III. **21:** Univ. Archives, College of William and Mary; Dartmouth College Library, Hanover, N.H., neg. no. 130la. **23:** Courtesy American Antiquarian Soc. **24, 25:** Map by Maryland CartoGraphics, Inc. **28, 29:** © 1995 David Muench. **30, 31:** © Allen Russell/Profiles West, Inc. **32, 33:** Jim Stamates. **34, 35:** © Allen Russell/Profiles West, Inc. **36, 37:** © Branson Reynolds/Profiles West, Inc. **40:** Cherokee National Hist. Soc., Tahlequah, Okla. **41:** Canadian Museum of Civilization, Hull, Que., no. 80-6681—*The National Archives of the United States* published by Harry N. Abrams, Inc., photo by Jonathan Wallen. **42:** Massachusetts Archives. **43:** New York Public Library—Univ. of Tulsa, McFarlin Library, Alice Robertson Collection. **46-49:** Missouri Hist. Soc. **50, 51:** Field Museum, neg. no. A14488; Missouri Hist. Soc. **52, 53:** Missouri Hist. Soc. **54, 55:** Missouri Hist. Soc., neg. no. LPE#1270; Field Museum, neg. nos. 15919—A15913. **56:** Missouri Hist. Soc., neg. no. WF#1053. **57:** Field Museum, neg. nos. A13594; 3600—13533. **58, 59:** Field Museum, neg. nos. 15127—15163; Missouri Hist. Soc., neg. no. WF#811. **60, 61:** Cat. no. 7720/12. Santa Clara Polished Plainware Train, 1900-1920. School of American Research Collections in Museum of New Mexico. Douglas Kahn, photographer; Heard Museum. **62:** Heard Museum. **63:** Heard Museum (2); cat. no. 46051. Navajo Early Yei Pattern Rug ca. 1900. Museum of Indian Arts & Culture/Laboratory of Anthropology, Santa Fe. Douglas Kahn, photographer. **64:** Heard Museum. **65:** Heard Museum—cat. no. 10814/12. Zuni Bear Carving ca. 1930. School of American Research Collections in Museum of New Mexico. Blair Clark, photographer; Heard Museum. **66,**

67: Heard Museum (2)—cat. no. 52967/12. Hopi Kachina doll 1930-1940, from the von Preissig and Bachrach Collection. Museum of New Mexico. Blair Clark, photographer. **68, 69:** Heard Museum (2); cat. no. 54211/12. Tesuque Figurine Rain God ca. 1900, gift of Rick Dillingham estate. Museum of New Mexico. Blair Clark, photographer; Judson Collection at Magic Lantern Castle Museum, San Antonio, Tex. **70, 71:** Library of Congress, RBR Negative 2746 of Broadside #240, #24—Archives and Manuscripts Division of Oklahoma Hist. Soc., no. 3910. **72:** Hampton Univ. Archives, Hampton, Va. **73:** Steve Tuttle, courtesy Ataloe Lodge, Bacone College, Muskogee, Okla.; State Hist. Soc. of North Dakota, no. MUS-603. **75:** National Anthropological Archives (NAA), Smithsonian Inst., no. 56185. **76, 77:** Special Collections, Univ. of Oregon Library, neg. no. M5588. **78:** *The Reservation Blackfeet, 1882-1945*, by William E. Farr. Univ. of Washington Press, Seattle, 1984. **79:** State Hist. Soc. of North Dakota, neg. no. 9969. **80:** Library of Congress, neg. no. USF-34-80943-E. **81:** Library of Congress, no. USZ-62-55633; Library of Congress. **82:** From "Buffalo Bill's Wild West" program, courtesy Buffalo Bill Hist. Center, Cody, Wyo.; State Hist. Soc. of North Dakota. **83:** State Hist. Soc. of North Dakota, neg. no. A-5668. **84, 85:** Buffalo Bill Hist. Center, Cody, Wyo.; Wyoming State Museum, Stimson Collection, 1860. **86, 87:** Photographer Edward Truman, courtesy Denver Public Library, Western History Dept.—Buffalo Bill Hist. Center, Cody, Wyo., neg. no. P.69.972; Buffalo Bill Hist. Center, Cody, Wyo., neg. no. P.69.831—photo courtesy National Museum of the American Indian (NMAI), Smithsonian Inst., neg. no. P13677. **88, 89:** Photo by Thomas Magee, Sherburne Collection, Univ. of Montana, on loan to William E. Farr—Montana Hist. Soc., gift of John W. Blair (2)—from *The Way to Independence*, by Carolyn Gilman and Mary Jane Schneider. Minnesota Hist. Soc. Press, St. Paul, 1987. **90:** Cumberland County Hist. Soc., Carlisle, Pa. **91:** Hampton Univ. Archives, Hampton, Va. **92:** NAA, Smithsonian Inst., no. 53502. **93:** NAA, Smithsonian Inst., no. 53413-C. **94:** Trudy W. Pearson. **97:** Minnesota Hist. Soc., neg. no. 42854. **98:** Minnesota Hist. Soc., neg. no. 32977. **99:** NAA, Smithsonian Inst., no. 43583. **101:** Archives and Manuscripts Division of Oklahoma Hist. Soc., no. 7960. **102, 104:** Photo by John Anderson, Jack R. Williams Collection. **105:** Photo courtesy NMAI, Smithsonian Inst., cat. no. 2/1673. **106:** Univ. of Colorado Museum at Boulder. **107:** Courtesy NMAI, Smithsonian Inst., cat. nos. 19/3217; 12/2259. **108:** Hampton Univ. Museum, Hampton, Va.—courtesy Montana Hist. Soc. **109:** Courtesy Montana Hist. Soc. (2); Museum of Indian Arts & Culture, photo by Douglas Kahn. **110, 111:** *The Reservation Blackfeet, 1882-1945*, by William E. Farr. Univ. of Washington Press, Seattle, 1984—Olga Ross Hannon Collection #1126, Montana State Univ., courtesy William E. Farr. **112, 113:** Alaska State Library, Case and Draper Collection, neg. no. PCA 39-15; courtesy Royal British Columbia Museum, Victoria, neg. no. PN 8745. **114:** Trans. no. 4741 (2), courtesy Dept. of Library Services, American

Museum of Natural History. **115:** State Hist. Soc. of North Dakota. **116:** From *Irredeemable America*, Imre Sutton, Univ. of New Mexico Press, 1985. **117:** Maps by Maryland CartoGraphics, Inc. **119:** NAA, Smithsonian Inst., no. 1434-A. **120:** Hampton Univ. Archives, Hampton, Va. **121:** Hampton Univ. Museum, Hampton, Va.—Hampton Univ. Archives, Hampton, Va. (2). **122:** Hampton Univ. Archives, Hampton, Va. **123:** Hampton Univ. Museum, Hampton, Va.—Hampton Univ. Archives, Hampton, Va. **124:** Hampton Univ. Archives, Hampton, Va.—Hampton Univ. Museum, Hampton, Va. **125-128:** Hampton Univ. Archives, Hampton, Va. **129:** Courtesy Pennsylvania Academy of the Fine Arts, Philadelphia—Hampton Univ. Archives, Hampton, Va.; Hampton Univ. Museum, Hampton, Va. (2). **130:** Hampton Univ. Archives, Hampton, Va. **131:** Nebraska State Hist. Soc.—Hampton Univ. Archives, Hampton, Va. **132:** Hampton Univ. Archives, Hampton, Va. **133:** Hampton Univ. Archives, Hampton, Va.—Hampton Univ. Museum, Hampton, Va. **134:** Courtesy Dennis Sanders, Hardin, Mont. **136, 137:** Courtesy Edward E. Ayer Collection, Newberry Library—National Archives, neg. no. RG75-M-3. **138:** NAA, Smithsonian Inst., no. 76-15853. **139:** National Archives, neg. nos. 1115687734 (708); 111SC87805 (733). **140:** NAA, Smithsonian Inst., no. 3404-6-1; Nevada Hist. Soc. **141:** National Archives, neg. no. 111SC87.749 (718); NAA, Smithsonian Inst., no. 53534. **142:** NAA, Smithsonian Inst., no. 214.821-A; South Dakota Hist. Soc. **143:** Archives & Manuscripts Division of Oklahoma Hist. Soc., no. 9615.45.E; National Archives, neg. no. 111SC87728 (704). **144:** Photo by Milton Snow of the Indian Service from a book by Donald L. Parman, *The Navajos and the New Deal*; South Dakota Hist. Soc. **145:** National Archives, neg. no. 111SC101530 (860). **146, 147:** Background © Eric Haase. Maps by Maryland CartoGraphics, Inc; South Dakota Hist. Soc. **150:** State Hist. Soc. of North Dakota. **151:** Edward Truman, courtesy Denver Public Library, West-ern History Dept. **152:** Photo by John Anderson, Jack R. Williams Collection. **153:** Montana Hist. Soc. **156:** Courtesy Osage Tribal Museum, Pawhuska, Okla., copied by Don Wheeler, Tulsa, Okla. **157:** NMAI, Smithsonian Inst. **159:** Eastern Washington State Hist. Soc., Spokane, Wash. **160, 161:** Courtesy Southwest Museum, Los Angeles, photo. no. N.24912; National Archives, neg. no. RG 75-PU-WA-56. **165:** Library of Congress, neg. no. USZ-62-41717. **166:** *The Reservation Blackfeet, 1882-1945*, by William E. Farr. Univ. of Washington Press, Seattle, 1984. **167:** James Willard Schultz papers, Montana State Univ., Bozeman. **168:** Delores Twohatchet. **169:** Bettmann Archive. **172, 173:** Western History Collections, Univ. of Oklahoma Library; *The Reservation Blackfeet, 1882-1945*, by William E. Farr. Univ. of Washington Press, Seattle, 1984. **175:** National Archives, neg. no. NA75N-Misc-(115). **176, 177:** Map by Maryland CartoGraphics, Inc.; © Eric Haase/CPI. **178, 179:** © Allen Russell/Profiles West, Inc. **180, 181:** © Eric Haase/CPI (2); © Allen Russell/Profiles West, Inc. **182, 183:** Ted Wood Photography. **184, 185:** Ted Wood Photography (3); © Allen Russell/Profiles West, Inc.